Democracy and Democratic Institutions in Social Transformation

21st Century Perspective

All India Progressive Forum (AIPF)

President
Prof. K.S. Chalam (M) 077022 00026
chalamks@hotmail.com

Working President
M. Vijaya Kumar (M) 098489 33545
marlavk@yahoo.com

General Secretary
Anil Rajimwale (M) 098685 25812
anilrajim@gmail.com

Democracy and Democratic Institutions in Social Transformation

21st Century Perspective

Edited by
Krishna Jha

AAKAR

Proceedings of the Workshop held on December 31, 2013 to January 2, 2014 at Jawaharlal Nehru University, New Delhi

First Published 2018

ISBN 978-93-5002-533-8 (Hb)

Published by
AAKAR BOOKS
28 E Pocket IV, Mayur Vihar Phase I,
Delhi 110 091 India
aakarbooks@gmail.com

in association with
All India Progressive Forum
New Delhi

Laser Typeset at
Arpit Printographers, Delhi 110 032

Printed at
Mudrak, Delhi 110 091

Contents

General Secretary's Note

AIPF has been holding workshop-cum-seminars regularly for the last eight years. It has already published the proceedings of the first workshop on 21st Century Socialism. The present volume on Democracy and Democratic Institutions, held in New Delhi from December 31, 2013 to January 2, 2014, is the second one in the series of publication of proceedings, edited by Krishna Jha. We intend to bring out the proceedings of all the workshops. Unfortunately owing to a number of technical and other unavoidable reasons, we have been unable to arrange them in the chronological yearly order. Therefore, we will publish them when they are ready.

The responsibility to bring out the proceedings of all the workshops has been given to Krishna Jha, the general editor for the series, who is also an NEC (National Executive Committee) member. She has done an excellent job of finalizing the present volume under the most trying conditions despite her very busy schedule.

Democracy is a most important question in India and the world over in the present context and in the background of the new technological and information revolution. The workshop has tried to carry forward the discussion, emphasizing emerging features under the influence of new sciences and technologies. The discussion continues even outside the framework of the workshop.

A number of prominent academicians, scholars, activists and youth took part in thorough and frank debates and exchange of opinions. We are grateful to them for their enlightening contributions. Comments and suggestions are welcome. The editor's phone number and email are meationed.

New Delhi, **Anil Rajimwale**
October 21, 2017

Editor's Note

The workshop on 'Democracy and Democratic Institutions in Social Transformation: 21st Century Perspective' was intended to take up the themes with the emerging analytical tools, developing under the strong influence of STR and ICR that play a decisive role today.

In the years after the Second World War, finance capital had almost taken hold of the territorial division and was moving towards dividing the market. These shifts indicated not only the growing role of finance capital, but also its clear division with the productive capital. It also had a tendency to acquire economic and political hegemony. This was expressed in the rise of fascism, that was defeated by the forces of democracy and socialism, a new beginning to deter the growth of finance capital. It was also a time when new democratic institutions started emerging and matured by the 21stcentury as parliamentary and constitutional institutions, standing guard against the right wing forces that represented the interest of finance capital. Today such forces have emerged stronger in the Latin American countries and in several other regions.

Brazil has been an example of the same. Back in 1973, Chile had emerged as an example of the use of parliamentary institutions for radical changes when the left and democratic forces won the elections. Though soon after it got crushed by the dictatorship of finance capital. Vietnam was another example of socialist and democratic forces joining together in the struggle. It was the entire people that fought against the colonial forces led by great giants like the US and France among others. It was the victory of the forces of democracy and socialism.

Today, as the economic crisis deepens, there is no interruption in the development of the means of production and that brings in the role of STR and ICR. This has brought the productive growth to a new stage, a stage that has been a total shift from whatever was.

The revolution in the mode of production has also created a need for change in the superstructure and in the democratic and parliamentary institutions. STR and the ICR need democratic institutions and hence democracy emerges widespread and strong, as it never was.

Despite the growing role of the finance capital, and the forces of imperialism, along with STR and ICR, development of capitalism continues, perhaps not so much in large-scale production, but certainly in small and medium-scale production, along with the growing service sector.

The democratic forces have to reign in these potentials, and make them serve the common masses. Eradication of unemployment is one such goal.

Also at this stage, the growing concentration of wealth and capital has to be observed in its unity and contradiction. As capital grows powerful, it also becomes non-capital, since it is non-existent, and cannot take part in the production process. The developed world has become the victim of this crisis. They do not have productive capital while the developing world strives to perfect production.

It is this division between the forces of speculative capital and the productive capital that has to be removed. The fabric of the democratic programme has to be woven around this initiative.

With this objective, themes have been dealt with.

The base paper, by Anil Rajimwale, itself traces the path our own country has traversed in the pre and post-independence period. He says, "Today, we have a vast and widespread network of democratic institutions from parliamentary to the village levels, and horizontally too: universities, colleges, social and cultural institutions. That these institutions have played a stellar role in developing the socio-economic and political prowess as well as building democratic consciousness creating a flexible psyche is evidenced by the whole post-independence history. Without democracy, India would not be what it is today. One cannot imagine India without its vast network of democratic institutions and without a deeply-rooted democratic consciousness."

Also a distinction is drawn deliberately in the paper between 'old' and 'new' technology, because it does not want to be confined to discussing issues only in relation with the industrial revolution but also, and much more, with the new, with electronics, information and the broader scientific and technological revolution or the STR. Capitalism is basically a product of the industrial revolution, he writes and adds that it was capitalism which led the anti-feudal revolution, paving the way for capitalist relations of production and for modern democracy. Here he makes one of his unique observations, saying that it was capitalism that ushered in the new, industrial revolution, as it needed its own production structure.

Another piece by Soma Marla, analysing 'Modern Technology and the Working Class in the Era of Neoliberal Capitalism', says, "Before capitalism productive forces were growing slowly and hence developments in production were slow and gradual. Manufacturing today is very technology intensive and capitalism is adopting it instantly. The technology today is mainly based on silicon chips, fibre optics, satellite communications, robots and factory shop floor automation. Capitalism needs science and technology to expand production, create new products, generate more surplus value, thereby to make big profits. In the present technology paradigm, it is interesting to analyse how modern science and technology are serving society, affecting the working class, employment, trade union rights, consciousness and finally the class struggle."

In yet another piece, while dealing with the perspective of democracy today, C.R. Bakshi writes, "This is what is exactly necessary to be done in India today—prepare for genuine democratic revolution, through agitations, propaganda and exposure of capitalist loot of resources and wealth of the nation. All the left parties with their ideology of socialism should join hands with those democrats who are committed to 'sovereignty, socialism and secularism', the goal of Indian democracy as has been solemnly resolved, to build a strong joint movement for necessary amendments in the Constitution, to implement the Directive Principles of State Policy in letter and spirit."

With realistic optimism, M. Vijaya Kumar in his piece observes: "We should not forget that technology by itself cannot bring about a change, but the application of these tools of technology for an intended constructive purpose, can only become an agent of change. And the physical conditions for this phenomenon have emerged in recent times."

Discussing the new shift, in the context of STR and ICR, Krishna Jha notes, "In the process of capitalist development, emerges the social individual, harbinger of the new society. The substitution of science for labour as the chief force of production is inevitable as Marx pointed out, capital calls to life all the powers of science and nature ... in order to make creation of wealth independent (relatively) of the labour time employed in it."

While discussing socialism, STR and social revolution in India, Ramesh Rattan affirms, "The slogan of socialism, after 70 years of its existence and changing the civilization on this planet in an unprecedented manner, has lost its guiding and inspiring shine. The command system with the centralized economy could not meet the aspirations of the people adopting it. On the other hand, the theory of free economy propounded by capitalists is facing a crisis on such a scale that most of the people on this globe want to change this mode of production/distribution which exploit our natural resources in a ruthless manner and causing a lot of misery to the wider section of toiling masses."

Writing about ICR, S.K. Roy observes, "People who have an interest in current political issues and the capacity to learn about them now have access to the information they need to be equipped to make an impact on public policy. Using online tools to organize, people can more easily be involved in the policy-making process of government. The first impact has also led to more public engagement efforts. Government officials are pressured by more highly informed, opinionated, and potentially effective citizens to make a further effort to address the public's concerns."

Bharat Bhushan Prasad has written about the hitherto path of democracy and its changing features in the 21st century. He has also noted the changes that it would have on the masses.

Aravind Kumar has made observations about democracy, socialism and characterizing democracy. He has analysed the changing connotation of 'People' when he says, "If democracy refers to a 'rule of the people' then whom does the word 'people' refer to, whether it refers to the exploiting classes like capitalists, landlords or the exploited ones like workers, toilers, or in simple terms 'working masses'? For Marx and Engels it included only the 'working masses', and it is thus that the meaning and operation of democracy must change with the changing nature of the word 'people'."

To prohibit the growing awareness, efforts are made to divide the 'people', destroying the composite character of their culture, and there the role of communalism finds a place.

Ganesh has made powerful observations in this context.

Thus the effort was summed up finally as an immense success. The collection is an effort to reflect this success. But the main handicap faced was lack of written papers, though discussions were lively and animated.

Krishna Jha
Email: whereiskrishna@gmail.com
(M) 9350898714

1

Democracy and Democratic Institutions in Social Formation: 21st Century Perspective

Yugal Rayalu

With a long history of many turbulences and travails, and after a prolonged struggle for independence, the wise people of this great land chose to make India a modern secular state that would guarantee equality to all people irrespective of gender, caste, religion and region.

The foundation of the modern Indian state is an equally modern Constitution which has shaped the destiny of all Indians over the past six decades. The preamble of our Constitution starts with:

> We the people of India ...Give to ourselves this Constitution...

At a stroke of the pen the injustices of thousands of years have been theoretically dispensed with. On day one of the adoption of the Constitution men and women became equal as far as the state was concerned. Women got their voting rights from the very first day.

Our Constitution has no mention of any god, caste or religion. It speaks of all the people as equal citizens. People are addressed as the masters and also as the servants of this great country. Rights are mentioned along with duties and responsibilities.

The Preamble to the Constitution of India very clearly indicates the philosophy of the direction which India is supposed to follow. It is a most scientifically developed document accepted by all Indians, ushering this ancient land into a path of peace and development. Our Constitution is the foundation of our democratic institutions. Naturally the Constitution of India must be revered by all of us.

One of the most important gifts of the Constitution of India is to the marginalized sections of society. Millions of those who were always asked to live outside the periphery of "respectable" society, were given equal and dignified status from day one. In a major development, one citizen, one vote principle was adopted so that in a sense all citizens would feel that sense of equality.

Democracy is the institution that guarantees these rights to all the otherwise marginalized sections of society. It is very important that the institutions of democracy remain strong so that the fruits of development reach the weakest. It is not an easy task to make democracy work vibrantly in a society which is mostly illiterate and backward. The affluent section would be only too happy to see democracy fail and falter. The powerful minuscule section would be glad to see the end of this new institution called democracy. It is most backward and the weak sections of the society who are benefited by democracy and hence the responsibility of saving and revitalizing democracy rests on their shoulders.

The arrival of democracy is no small happening in a country like India. It is not less than a revolution, that yesterday's untouchables are part of the ruling apparatus of modern India. A few years ago they were not allowed to touch books.

There are many failures of democracy in India. Corruption has set in. Lethargy is a major problem. Regionalism, fundamentalism, casteism and obscurantism have all entered our institutions from the back door. Frankly speaking, these are not the failures of the institution of democracy. These are the failures of the players of democracy. A society where half the population cannot read and write, where a part of the society is homeless, where a girl child is killed before she could be born, survival of democracy for six decades, is a big achievement. It is almost a miracle that in such a state, the transfer of power is very smooth, which never happened in the entire history of India. It goes to the credit of the institutions of democracy that peace prevails in the country despite all the efforts of the trouble mongers. Even if the peace that prevails is fragile, it is still precious. Likewise the dilapidated yet surviving institutions of democracy are a thousand times better than any institutions of dictatorship or any other form of governance.

Indian institutions of democracy have matured over the years. The path they traversed was not always smooth. The old mindsets repeatedly tried every small opportunity to malign the modern idea of universal franchise and equality before the law. It goes to the credit of the common man and woman of this great country that the institutions of people who owned and managed public utility have survived the onslaughts of feudal mindsets and threats from the powerful capitalist class.

Political parties with different ideologies are the main torch bearers of democracy in India. The most important task of these political parties is to strengthen the foundations of democracy. The supremacy of the Constitution must be accepted by all. Our Constitution is not a belief or a dogma. It is a dynamic document in practice with the provisions of change wherever and whenever needed. It transcends all boundaries of caste, creed and community. It is outside the boundaries of religions. It does not interfere in any one's faith and does not allow any faith to interfere. This sanctity of the Constitution must be maintained at all costs.

It is the duty of the enlightened and the learned to take the message of democracy and its institutions to the vast majority of this great country. People of India have been participating in the democratic exercise of electing governments very religiously. The need of the hour is to take this participation to a further level where the decision-making and implementation are affected.

Democracy is the new way of life in India now. Every part of our social life is now affected by democratic norms. From temple trusts to educational institutions, all social organizations now function on the principles of democracy. This is the new reality.

In spite of the fact that democracy has developed deep roots in our socio-political life, there are some forces that malign democracy. These are the forces from the ultra right, ulta left and the religious fundamentalists. Basically these people are against modernity. They oppose everything that is based on scientific understanding of the world. These people have a feudal mindset and hence continue to live in the past. They are the prisoners of their stagnant minds. The pioneers of our Constitution had to fight a prolonged battle with these outdated minds. Fortunately for us the modern minds could win so that we have an egalitarian Constitution that does not discriminate between two human beings.

On one hand we have the battle against these feudal minds, and on the other hand we have to fight against the stooges of capitalism, who try to subvert people's power in the name of efficiency and profitability. Using the most modern communication tools these stooges poison the young minds to wean them away from the path of struggle. They call politics dirty yet always use the power of politics to forward and pursue their own agenda! The challenge to democracy comes from these so-called modern sections of society. The battle with these modern pirates has to be fought with more modern tools of technology and communication. We need to save democracy from the clutches of these servants of the moneyed class.

The only way to defeat the negative designs of the enemies of democracy is to encourage increasing participation from the working class. Unity of the working class is the best defence against money and muscle power. Numerically the working class is far superior to the minuscule owner class. Only a vigilant working class can defeat the enemies of democracy.

As Lenin has famously said,

> The working class without knowledge is powerless. With knowledge the working class is a powerful force.

The state apparatus at present is intended to keep the majority away from the power of education. Formal higher education is becoming more and more costly. The marginalized sections of society are needed to be educated about their rights informally. An educated proletariat is a force to reckon with. Their participation in democracy and all the democratic processes will enrich the social fabric of society. This participation will make our democracy really strong and the institutions of democracy will become dynamic in the real sense.

(This presentation was the keynote address at the workshop)

2

Democracy and Democratic Institutions in Social Transformation: 21st Century Perspective

Anil Rajimwale

India is a unique experiment in democracy and democratic institutions since early independence. It is the only country in the world, which imparted universal adult franchise to its entire population with one stroke of the pen on the very day its Constitution (January 26, 1950) was implemented, irrespective of class, caste, religion, sex, literacy, rich or poor. It was something that took other countries decades and centuries to achieve.

Evolution of the Parliamentary Constitutional System

One of the distinguishing features of Indian democracy is that the struggle for parliamentary institutions and right to vote was part of the Indian freedom movement. The right to vote was selective and depended on the economic status during the British rule. People with money power were preferred. Thus the right to vote was available to only a very small section of the population. Yet, the democratic rights continued to expand, however slowly, under mass pressure of the freedom struggle and constitutional movements and in this direction, 1919, 1935, 1937, 1946, etc. constituted major landmarks towards the constitutional freedom of the Indian people. Despite the restrictions on the voting rights, Indians achieved major gains in the general elections of 1937, when the Indian National Congress came to power in nine out of eleven provinces, supported en masse by the poor and the landless. That opened the limited field of democratic freedoms for workers, peasants, students, industrialists, intelligentsia and other sections to further press for their rightful demands.

1946 was another major landmark in the sense that it established a Constituent Assembly to form a government to oversee the transfer of power and to work out a Constitution for independent India. Formation of the workers' constituencies was an important achievement of the period, which sent several workers' representatives to the elected bodies.

Thus, our constitutional and democratic structure has a major history and long period of struggle behind it. It is often forgotten that we fought as much for political freedom as for the democratic, parliamentary and constitutional rights.

Today, we have a vast and widespread network of democratic institutions from parliamentary to the village levels, and horizontally too: universities, colleges, social and cultural institutions.

That these institutions have played a stellar role in developing the socio-economic and political prowess as well as building democratic consciousness creating a flexible psyche is evidenced by the whole post-independence history. Without democracy India would not be what it is today. One cannot imagine India without its vast network of democratic institutions and without a deeply rooted democratic consciousness.

The difference will at once become clear if we look at our neighbouring countries, where due to insufficient democracy, the masses and the democratic forces are not able to assert themselves, and where therefore the reactionary backward-looking forces dominate and dictate.

India's economic development, evolving around a powerful public sector, has been possible because of a strong democracy.

India is unique also in the sense that in no other country do we find so many political varieties and governments run by different parties and political combinations in different states and in the centre at the same time. And yet, India as a unity in diversity not only survives but continues to gain strength. It is the strength of democracy, not of dictatorship.

That is why the enemies of India want to weaken and destroy precisely this strong democratic system which is the main source of strength. It can only be improved, not destroyed.

Other Democratic Institutions

Besides the parliamentary and such other electoral bodies, India has a widespread and advanced network of other kinds of democratic institutions. Among them is the growing media network, that perhaps no other country has. Every state and almost every district and local area has daily and other newspapers, magazines, periodicals, journals and such others in various languages with a rich variety, and they keep growing. There is no other country which has periodicals in so many languages and of so many varieties. In addition, the electronic media keeps increasing and spreading, playing a key role in consciousness formation.

Our country has a vast network of socio-economic and political institutions, organizations and parties.

Democratic Rights

India has a long tradition of struggle for democratic rights since the days of the British rule. After independence, these rights have vastly extended and expanded, playing a crucial role in improving the conditions of the people. The rights include those of expression of views and their propagation, free press, agitation and assembly, open protests against injustices, strikes, demonstrations and processions. Many mass movements and agitations take place spontaneously as well as by various political and non-political organizations. They help to improve our system and expand our consciousness. Indians are among the most conscious, socially and politically alert and creative people.

We have a highly intricate network, for example, of the labour and industrial laws. There is a powerful and active trade union movement and an effective labour-industrial machinery, which has recently been under attack from the vested interests. The public sector workers and their organizations play a crucial role in the process of economic and political democratization, and they are the base of the entire economy and politics. We have a progressive working class, whose role is often underestimated in the building of the nation and the national economy. The public sector has also been the target of backward looking forces, both inside and outside the country.

1969 was a crucial year when the progressive forces of the country took a giant step by nationalizing the biggest monopoly banks, taking away the privy purses of the princely houses and instituting all round political, economic and social reforms. Such a working class contributed to the strengthening of the political and civil society. There can be no talk of a civil society in India without the industrial working class with the public sector employees as its core. If there has been further and diversified growth, it has been possible only due to and based on the public sector.

The public sector basically has contributed to the creation of the infrastructure and heavy machine base of India's economy, and thus to the political stability and strengthening. In other words, the public sector is the most democratizing force in India. It is a pity that it is being ignored and attacked from various extreme corners. If India is united, sovereign and independent, it is because of the railways, communications, oil and gas, electricity, power, roads, communications including the electronic one, water and irrigation, defence and so on. The political and other economic structures are a fall-out of this phenomenon.

For the first time, we find a working class without a direct capitalist class, and with participation in management, however limited. These facts are of great long-term significance for the democratic transformation in the country in the direction of an equitable society.

Significance of Democracy for People and Nation

The point here is that these rights and democratic institutions are crucial aspects of our lives. They have to be preserved against all the odds, threats and attacks. If we look at those countries which have only incipient or undeveloped democracies or none at all, we can understand the great and even crucial importance of democratic institutions for our life. Some of the neighbouring countries and even those at a distance suffer terribly because of either absence or a weak democracy and democratic institutions. Every effort is being made to prevent their evolution in those countries.

Today, democracy has become a weapon in the hands of the people, who have changed governments at will in the various states and in the centre. Besides, our Constitution and the democratic institutions can be used to bring about basic and people-oriented transformations.

Our Constitution clearly states that our country is republican, democratic, secular and socialist. In other words, it has tremendous inherent potential.

The question is whether we have made full use of this system and its potential to transform the country, the life of the people, create a new socio-economic entity and democratize consciousness. Tolerance for dissent and views of others, respect for various religions and their cooperation for the good of society and to change it, and such other aspects are some of the axial features of our lives, personal and social.

So, democracy is not just a system of political and social institutions. *It is the very way of life.* It is the way we live, work, discuss and debate. It is a new kind of social discourse. Tolerance, cooperation and respect for each other, a social consent to differ and debate and come together in a historical bloc to form the central social and democratic matrix which determine our consciousness. A historical bloc and maximum consent on minimum common issues should be the methodology to go forward along the path of progress.

So, democracy is *the culture of human interaction and mutual respect*, and not just a political system. *Democracy is a new form of culture.*

It is regrettable that even in the 21st century we come across tendencies that question the very basic principle of democracy, that weaken democratic consciousness, that do not like and respect dissent, that want to threaten and even destroy the hard-won democratic institutions and rights won through struggles of centuries. They are actually afraid of forward-looking and progressive democratic ideas of humanism and social change through peaceful democratic consent. They threaten the very concept of democracy.

The Spirit: Assimilation of Democracy

Democracy is not something that we just use for our purpose. Of course, democracy is 'useful' and 'good'. But it is much more. The very spirit of democracy has to be assimilated. It is the way we live, think and act. It should become a habit. There are people and groups who come to power through democratic means, yet they do not have full faith in it. They discard it the moment they are in place. This way they discard the people themselves who put them in positions of power.

If one does not have complete faith in the Indian Constitution and its basic principles, one will do nothing for the people. The parliamentary system has to perform, but if no work is discharged, then it is bound to be paralyzed. It is not enough to come to power; it is also essential to use the system in favour of the people. If a particular party, for example, is elected but does nothing for the economy, society and people under the alibi that 'nothing can be done', then not only does the party go out of power but the constitutional system itself is weakened.

This is a dangerous trend. It shows that the democratic spirit and content has not really been assimilated. Democratic rights have been won after protracted struggles, and they must not be frittered away; rather they should be strengthened and developed further.

Dimensions of Democracy

We need to study the details of various aspects of democracy, particularly keeping in view the peculiarities of the 21st century. We need to discuss and ponder over the significance of democratic institutions for social change in India, the role of various aspects and estates like the media and parties and structures, history of democracy and social justice and socialism, interpretations of socialism including those by Swami Vivekanand, the gender issue, new dimensions in the 21st century due to the STR and the ICR, whether postmodernism and post-industrialism help to expand democratic consciousness through new forms of discourse, great democratic role of electronics which cuts through all the barriers of the state, government, nations and classes, the outlines of a new world that is emerging globally, new and tremendous endless possibilities of solving basic, fundamental human problems and issues, meeting the new holistic and global problems of environment, renewable and sustainable energy that go beyond class questions, the participation of India in a new world democratic order, new forms of democratic and if some people like it, socialist transformations. Many more issues constitute the endless dimensions of democracy. There could be many interpretations of democracy, social change, socialism, and humanism.

21st Century, STR and Democracy

The scientific and technological revolution or STR has opened new theoretical and practical horizons for democracy, so much so that democracy itself needs quantitative and qualitative rearrangement to be reidentified and redefined. The information and communication revolution or the ICR, a by-product of the STR, has begun redefining the dimensions of our thought and practice, deepening and expanding their democratic content.

The STR is a momentous event as far as democracy is concerned. It has opened new horizons and new pathways for democracy and social transformations in the 21st century by providing new means in the hands of every individual. The role of the subject/individual has increased as never before. What is interesting and important is that the electronics revolution is creating absolutely novel democratic structures, tools and means.

The STR/ICR enhance the place and role of information, which is a key factor in a truly democratic system. We are living in a world of a stream of information, images and knowledge. Computers, internet and mobiles are creating a world of information. The planet earth is being surrounded by increasing layers of information waves. Information is available at the press of a button or key. This is a great democratic advance. Electronics have speeded up and accelerated the participation of the people and individuals in the affairs of society.

Parties, governments, states, countries and nations, are all going through changes under the impact of faster information and its tools. The speed and nature of the decision-making process is changing and becoming faster. Decisions have to be taken quickly and concretely. There are features which do not fit in with the traditional ones. The state has become a relative entity, for the control of which the parties vie with each other. Certain features are exemplified by the European state.

The borderline between the civil and political society becomes less clear and more inter-penetrative and inter-active. The state is now more than a class organization. The governments and the parties act more as managing agencies/organizations, if they can use information properly.

Information plays an instant role in the consciousness formation. It increases people's role. At the same time, it is fraught with dangerous and harmful tendencies of erroneous and faulty decision-making.

Parties, the state, government and political structures *display certain postmodern and post-industrial* characteristics.

The means, tools and equipment created by the STR are individual-savvy and therefore have the potentials of more direct democracy. The role of the subject has increased as never before. Media, internet, electronics, computers, TV, etc and in particular mobiles are transforming the way we think and work.

The STR has reversed the tendencies in the development of the means of production on several counts. The most important, it is reducing the size of machines and the tools, creating tremendous possibilities for the expansion and spread of democracy. More can be produced by smaller means growing smaller in less time and smaller spaces by fewer people, creating more time and space for democracy. Thus, the collapse of space and time produce conditions for democratic revolution through step by step democratic transformations. It is a historic shift unleashed by the STR which cannot be stopped.

The source lies in the electron and electronic radiation and waves, which are getting converted into electronics as the historic means of production and information. No socio-economic and political institution can remain in tact in the face of the electrons and the particles. Therefore, this new particle is the most democratic ever created in human history.

The new particle has the inherent capacity to convert its energy into institutional energy whereby each individual can operate and convert the economic, social, political and ideological/theoretical forces. The electrons can penetrate the state, the government, the class and the party and engulf the world itself. It is a new tool of transformation that threatens everything that is history, converts everything into the past, makes obsolete the entire history, and begins new history/ies.

Factories and machines get smaller and their control comes into the hands of groups and individuals through simple hand-operated equipment which are worker-friendly. The factory and the industry collapse into a small computerized system with immense and unlimited democratic potential.

Mobiles and small hand-operated systems indicate the

trend towards the future. They contain an entire future society wherein the subject or the person can manipulate the world according to the laws of electronics. Therefore, the laws of society need to follow in the wake and transform or modify themselves.

The electron and electronics are nearer to the mind than anything that human beings have ever created. It is an unnatural force which has become a social force. Hence there are the acute contradictions in all the fields, which are the contradictions of development and not exactly of 'crisis'.

The electron (the particle) is democratic in its sheer speed and because it can carry information before anything else. Information in constant speed overturns the state and society and converts them into a coalition of ideas and forces for change. They are forced to change. If there is an instant communication with somebody at the other end of the earth, the intervening socio-political structures are cut through or by-passed. From then on, the further development of the superstructure diverts to make way for the electronically mediated communication. Thus, the greater such communications, the more obsolete the existing structures of society.

Therefore, part of democratization is the consideration of how to change the existing structures, organizations and parties in accordance with the rapid spread of electronics communication.

The rapid tendency towards smaller means of production and communication are assuming and going to assume new forms with greater democratic content in future. Among the developments of significance can be cited some of the following: nano-technology, genetic engineering, superconductivity, greater use of light energy, falling scales of the computers and mobiles, falling size of the micro-chip, etc. They are all democratic by nature. They have huge potentials to produce more materials and ideas (information) and thus of solving social problems. Production is no more a problem; the problem is now equitable distribution. Consequently, the structure of the society is bound to change as the conditions for democratic transformation are being created.

Typing has become the most democratic act today, and consequently everyone has become literate, at least potentially. It is no more simple writing; it is manipulating the object by subjectifying it. While in writing we simply write out our ideas, in and through typing we change the reality to one extent or the other. Typing gives commands which in turn means changing the reality according to our satisfaction. By the simple act of typing, we book a seat or add or delete or convert the industrial process.

This is possible because all the processes are converted into images, symbols, pictures, and streams on the screen. To operate the screen is to operate the world.

What is interesting and momentous is that all the hardware can and is being converted into software. This is the most revolutionary act of human history. That means humans are increasingly having command over natural and social processes.

Software, touch-screen and virtual realities have great potentials for the future of society and the individual, and also for democracy. One has to prepare for it by working out their implications. The borderline between software and hardware is getting blurred, and the hardware is losing the battle (contradiction) to software. Even the keyboard has already become part of software. This development is fraught with great possibilities for the future, as the machine, tools and other hard and tangible objects will be losing much of their present importance and role. *This has a direct bearing on democracy.*

Civil and Political Societies

India has a vast terrain or ground for exchange of views and ideas. Unfortunately, this rich texture of ideas has not been explored properly. In that sense in India reality is truly democratic where various ideas coexisted, interacted and constituted a united front of progressive and democratic ideas. Progress has been the base on which India's freedom struggle was fought, generating a wide range of rich ideas. The freedom movement was itself a wide front of ideas, movements and ideologies, where they interacted and cooperated. In a certain sense it was a historical bloc. Progressive ideas dominated. Traditions and practices of consent, cooperation, coexistence, freedom for dissent, and for creative development of ideas became the hallmark of our democracy.

Post-independence India has developed a rich and varied civil society, which also has a political and cultural role. No section can be kept out of it, particularly the workers, peasants, landless labourers, growing middle class and intelligentsia. Every movement and activities of the labouring masses should get reflected in the media and policies. Unfortunately certain media circles with vested interests do not want to reflect on the common labouring people, who are the value producers and value circulators.

Along with direct labourers, a new middle class is rising rapidly, who are placed importantly and strategically in the centres of production, creation of information and knowledge, and policy-making. They are the new important sectors of society.

Urbanization is proceeding rapidly, new urban giant conglomerations are coming into being, and thus new driving forces and driving centres are emerging. They play a key role in democracy and the democratic revolution.

Democratic Revolution and Institutions

Thus, the broadest possible social alliance and front with consent on many basic issues are emerging. It is a new kind of historical bloc with STR and ICR as their base. Equipped with modern and postmodern gadgets, the new working class and middle classes are crystallizing ideas of further expansion of democracy.

Demcoracy has become a continuous process with constant shifts in the democratic direction.

The conflict of democracy is basically due to the fact that we look at the new while being placed in the vantage point of the old. Our means of production and information are rooted in electronics but our mode of analysis and outlook is rooted in the industrial era. We try to fit the new into the old. Though our consciousness is evolving into the new world of images of electronics, we are cutting off that very consciousness as independent and as part of the industrial consciousness.

Dangers and Uncertainties

The democratic process is not a smooth and automatic process. Anti-social and reactionary, backward looking forces are active too. They can and do use new technological means, rapid changes in social composition, crises and temporary problems, media blowing things out of proportion, failures of traditional, obscurantist and obsolete ideologies to create and sow confusion to further their anti-democratic agenda. They want to obscure democratic ideologies, create the impression that you can move ahead without clear ideas, theories and ideologies. They are particularly against new theories based on science and STR, and create certain confusion in people's minds. They want to present science as magic to solve problems, and thus take recourse to populism and mysticism.

They want to break the alliance between science as a productive force and the working masses, middle sections and civil society, and disrupt the unity and clarity of issues. Science and technology are sought to be relegated to the background. The masses are being fed with cheap 'tablets' of quick solutions without the help of organized, scientific and well-planned steps. This is a dangerous development which creates grounds for fascism.

One must be on guard against these tendencies. It must be kept in mind that the new science and technology can also be used to create nuclear bombs, star wars and pin-pointed destruction, and to distort mass consciousness on a wide scale.

While going ahead, we have to preserve our composite culture, civilization and rich tradition.

That is why it has become even more essential to preserve and develop democratic institutions in our country and all over the world. We need to discuss how to use them. The 21st century is one of gigantic changes in all fields, rendering society free of the past and the outdated. We need to grow out into the 21st century and to bring the 22nd century into this century itself.

Without this futuristic as well as realistic feature, we cannot hope to transform our society and the world society and liberate ourselves from the age-old shackles.

We should therefore struggle to democratize everything including our very existence. We have to create the broadest possible front, cooperation and unity or simultaneous joint collaborative actions to create a new scenario and convert or give up the old. This effort has to base itself, not on some free-fall utopian non-scientific ideas on the pretext of 'democratic' ideas, but on deep and wide scientific and technological ideas. Democracy is not anarchy and a collection of thoughtless, most subjective utopian, non-scientific notions and ideas. It is not a wild celebration, dissemination and propaganda of senseless promises to 'do good to the people', as if people are waiting for charity.

It has to be clearly understood that today democracy is closely related to science and technology, with scientific theory. Without science and technology, there can be no real and stable democracy. Reversing Darwinism and taking human beings into the age of and stage of monkeys is certainly not democracy.

Therefore democracy is a scientific philosophy, an ideology, based on STR/ICR.

Democracy is not an empty promise but a promise or promises based on well-thought out, scientific studies with clear-cut futuristic plans. It is not confined to eating, drinking, jobs, water, electricity and housing, which of course are very important. Much more, democracy is about how to utilize and further develop science, technology, genetics, quantum mechanics, particle's motions, waves, electronics, etc., of how to enter a new world of post-industrial dispensation with science as the productive force. Democracy is about using the futuristic sciences and technologies, energy resources, freedom from pollution and preservation of environment for the good of individuals, society, in fact all living beings, and the earth itself.

Preservation of Environment and Ecology

Among the most crucial questions is the preservation and cleaning up of the environment. The environment has become the single most important issue before humanity, and not only humanity but for the earth itself. Often it is said that humans are threatened by pollution and environmental degradation, as if we are not bothered about other living beings. This perhaps is the most undemocratic act. It expresses the selfish motives of human beings to save only their own skins, from ecological disasters. The fact is that humanity has the responsibility towards the preservation of all living beings and the earth itself. They should stop thinking of polluting other planets or bodies.

Environmental questions unite our entire humanity. Therefore, it is the most democratic problem and its solution the most democratic act. Never before is the united front of humanity so spread out and wide and pressing. It is a cross-class and cross-social question. It is a question that overcomes all the socio-economic and political-philosophical questions and overcomes every contradiction that besets society. It is therefore a unique democratic issue that redefines the path of development itself.

It is a question of the future of humanity.

The workshop is only a humble effort to discuss these questions, and is only a beginning.

(The paper was written as a base paper for the discussion at the workshop held at JNU, New Delhi.)

3

Democracy in the 21st Century and the Masses: An Observation

Bharat Bhushan Prasad

The theory of democracy was developed by Plato, a Greek philosopher, in the 5th century BC. With some modifications, this model was adopted by England in the 17th century and later by many other European countries. Now almost all over the world it has been adopted with some variations and governments in those countries function according to the laws of democracy. Here one important point to be noted is that while in the 5th century BC, the model was in practice, it could be adopted again in the 17th century only and by England. Why was it not adopted in between? One reason may be that it was the age of feudalism and kings used to head the state and rule over the populace. Naturally the option for kings could never be democracy. Probably this is why it was adopted only when the capitalist revolution first occurred.

But now another question arises as to why this model of governance was adopted by the capitalists. Regarding this, there is an explanation by a section of Marxist scholars that by adopting democracy, the capitalists won over people including peasants to their side, which helped them to defeat feudal lords and kings during the capitalist-cum-industrial revolution. They further argue that democracy means people's rule. So almost the entire population was mobilized to their side and the capitalist revolution was successful. According to these scholars, democracy in any capitalist society will be for capitalists only because the entire state apparatus along with newspapers, radio, etc. will be in their hands and the general public will be motivated to vote according to the wishes of the capitalists. So their hypothesis was that although it will look like democracy for the entire population but in reality it will be the rule of capitalists only.

This formulation may be true to a great extent, but it is not the whole story. It is a general observation that the government in any capitalist country has to take into account the wishes of the people at large. It is another matter whether they do it willingly or are forced by the situation. A recent example from the headquarters of capitalism, that is the USA can be cited here. Recently Obama's administration has implemented the general health insurance for the entire population of the USA and a substantial amount of money will be spent on it by the US government. More such examples can be cited. So in any democracy under capitalism, there is pressure from the general public also and in absolute terms it is not democracy for the capitalists only.

Another point is about the famous crisis of capitalism. It is a fact that capitalism has inbuilt contradictions within itself. The last two world wars are proof of that. Here again there is a strong argument that due to the internal contradictions of capitalism, major social changes took place in the 20th century only. In support of this it is argued that during and after the First World War the first socialist country, that is the USSR emerged. Similarly during the course of the Second World War and subsequently after that the socialist world got huge expansion. Although it is true to a great extent, but this is not the whole truth. For example, take the case of America's liberation from the British colonialists in 1776. At that time capitalism was in its nascent stage only and monopoly had not yet developed. So there was no question of the contradiction of capitalism. But even then the British government had to liberate America. Immediately after that, a modified version of democracy was adopted by them. So there must be another reason for this.

This point will become clearer if we go back to the decades of the 1950s and 1960s. During this period almost all Asian, African and Latin American countries adopted democracy after their decolonization. This is because political parties or organizations, who carried out the freedom struggle in these countries, got inspiration from the democratic form of governance, which was already working in European countries. At this point let us assume a hypothetical situation. Suppose Raje-Rajware (kings) of our country had formed an association and tried to free India from the British. In that situation they could not have succeeded. Actually the freedom struggle became successful because people thought that after the ouster of the British it would be democracy in the country ending colonial oppression. This is true for all the countries that were liberated from colonial rule.

Actually there is an inbuilt inspiration for the people within Plato's model of democracy. In 1776, when America was decolonized, there was already democracy in England. The same is true for India and other countries as well. So people of these countries, including emerging capitalists, were inspired by it and the result was their freedom from colonial rule.

If we look at India then we find a number of welfare measures, including MGNREGA implemented here. Undoubtedly it is due to direct or indirect public pressure. But sometimes public pressure takes qualitatively different dimensions. For example, in the decade of the 1970s, in a

Latin American country called Chile left forces became the dominating factor in the government through democratic elections only. But the capitalist forces there nullified that development violently and thousands were killed in the process. A similar tragedy took place in Indonesia in the 1980s.

Now take the cases of some Latin American countries like Brazil and Venezuela. In these countries the present governments came to power only through the democratic process. Now they are forcing local capitalists to part with a portion of their profit for public welfare schemes.

What one would like to stress here is that it is not true that democracy means rule of the capitalist class alone. So, the democratic path of social change is not to be written off.

Now let us come to the present time when the socialist block is no more and the trio of liberalization, privatization and globalization is already in action. As a result of all these policies, health and education facilities all over the world have become very costly. Owing to these developments, not only the poor section of society but the middle class is also in dire financial trouble.

Probably for this reason only public pressure was generated and the USA had to implement health insurance for the masses at the cost of the government. This pressure is not only in the USA. Now all over the world public pressure is mounting for more welfare measures. Even in our country, right to education, right to food, right to health, etc. have become slogans of ruling capitalist parties.

As mentioned, all positive points in favour of democracy are inspiring people in spite of many serious drawbacks of capitalism. The rule of democracy does not prescribe any particular economic model for society. Actually its idea of freedom and equality apply to the economy as well. In a democracy, everybody is free to be engaged in any economic activity according to his or her wish. There are no constraints on somebody becoming a millionaire or even bigger. The number of murders in a country can also indicate the drawbacks of democracy. For example, in the year 2006, there were 70,030 murders in the USA. Similarly, during the year 2009, there were 10,277 cases of rapes in France. But in spite of all this, there is another and better side in democracy, that is the very concepts of freedom and equality of ideas, that are very attractive to people in general.

Before concluding, one must mention the already collapsed socialist system led by the then USSR. In this connection first of all I would like to mention the following: in 1977, I was in Bulgaria, which was a communist ruled state at that time, for seven months and am aware of the situation there. In that country each person was directly or indirectly a government employee. Their salary was somewhere between 100 dollars and 400 dollars. Their standard of living was like any respectable government clerk in our country. The more important fact about them was that there was no crime at all. But even then that system failed. So it needs an explanation.

According to Hegel, a well-known German philosopher, although perception develops according to the concrete situation around the person, but there are certain factors that do not change at all. For example, there is the **survival instinct**. The survival instinct is the reference point that is a guiding element not only for a person but even for animals. This instinct will drive any person to become increasingly competent, which may drive him towards selfishness. Now take the case of any former socialist country, say the former USSR. Although basic requirements are fulfilled for every person of that country, he or she can not own a factory. S/he could not even imagine such a situation. But according to this reason he should continuously improve himself.

Under this formulation different types of hierarchy were created there. For example, there were separate shops for Communist Party members. Such a hierarchy was prevalent at different levels there. Although they succeeded in creating such hierarchies at different levels but they could not go beyond a level. This is because it would amount to going beyond the system. So they went beyond the to get their wishes fulfilled. Here it must be stressed that emergence of millionaires and billionaires, both in Russia and China are not accidents but according to the formulation of Hegel only.

So for them (citizens of any socialist country) personal ambitions were most important and to get them fulfilled they had to embarrass democracy. In other words, it can be said that democracy is more powerful than even the basic material needs.

So in conclusion, it can be said that in any democracy, the general mass is its important element and the institution of democracy cannot afford to ignore it.

4

Modern Technology and the Working Class in the Era of Neoliberal Capitalism

Soma S. Marla

Before capitalism productive forces were growing slowly and hence developments in production were slow and gradual. Manufacturing today is very technology intensive and capitalism is adopting it instantly. The technology today is mainly based on silicon chips, fibre optics, satellite communications, robots and factory shop floor automation. Capitalism needs science and technology to expand production, create new products, generate more surplus value, thereby to make big profits. In the present technology paradigm, it is interesting to analyse how modern science and technology are serving society, affecting the working class, employment, trade union rights, consciousness and finally the class struggle. Modern science and technology introduced two major changes, one is the new organization of labour process and the other is restructuring of the working day and wages paid. Capitalism has succeeded in accomplishing both these goals in India. Yet some questions remain:

1. Are modern science and technology serving society or capitalism?
2. Is technology imposing labour saving production?

3. Are the automation technologies really relieving workers of drudgery and providing more leisure and a better life?
4. Does introduction of new technology lead to polarization of wealth and poverty?
5. How do we deal with a scenario with expanded production, low wages, production 'without workers', high surplus value generation?
6. Can knowledge workers be considered as the scientific proletariat?
7. White collar vs blue collar, are the workers' numbers decreasing?

In the last century, labour (quantity of human labour) occupied a dominant part in the production of surplus value and self-valorization of capital. However in the current century the knowledge economy has brought fundamental changes in the capitalist mode of production. Knowledge has become a major productive force. It appears to be a dominant part of social activity in production of goods, and is determined not by labour, but by knowledge. That the exchange value of commodities is determined mainly by the content of the knowledge, information and intelligence that they contain. It becomes the principal source of value and profit.

The exchange value of a commodity in the market competes with other commodities defined by its technological superiority. The increasing qualitative character, less and less measurable of labour are redefining 'surplus labour' and 'surplus value' in current technology intensive production. The increase in labour productivity brought by introduction of technology into production (automatic assembly plants, silicon chips, fibre optics and satellite communications) results in reduction in necessary labour time, and, therefore, there is a rise in the number of unemployed.

Will Technology Lead to Labourless Production?

One of the means which capital used to extract was surplus value, through the development of science and technology. Today's automated assembly of automobile plants in Manesar or Greater Noida (Henry Ford's automation production line process) are designed to expand production and explicitly to break the power of the skilled workers and used as a weapon by capital to attack and break up concentrations of working class power.

Workers invest socially needed labour in production of commodities and thereby bring in 'Exchange Value'. If machines take away all the production activity and labour gets laid off in the process of production, there would not be any exchange value in the market for the produced commodities. As without exchange value there cannot be any profit, a capitalist can never totally remove workers from the production cycle.

Do Knowledge Workers Represent the Modern Proletariat?

Till the end of the last century, the dominant force of the working class was constituted of craftsmen and highly skilled engineering workers who provided the nucleus of industrial production. Even the latest technology is not very special, because it incorporates in its mode of operation the dexterity and skill of the workers while designing the advanced production. Technology, such as robotic automation only mimics human labour though with higher productivity. The worker himself is henceforth deprived of his/her skill and subordinated from the point of view of social production to that technology. Workers standing at an automated assembly plant or monitoring the computer screens are direct examples of these changes taking place on the shop floor today. Modern industry makes science a productive force distinct form labour and presses it into the service of capital. (Karl Marx).

Knowledge is a Result of Human Labour

As the army of scientists grow, the research activity also gets increasingly subjected to costs of production, and under interchangeability and managerial supervision, it can as well be treated as another variety of human labour, participating in commodity production. Thousands of scientists conducting experiments in laboratories, mathematicians and computer science professionals designing software scripts to develop innovative production technologies and more efficient tools could possibly be treated as knowledge workers in the production cycle.

As scientific activity is becoming quantified, capitalists can estimate in advance how much time it takes to come out with a new product design, how much labor and time are needed. It is a common practice in the automobile or pharmaceutical industry to forecast how much time it may take for development of a new automobile model or a new cancer drug. In the USA alone today there are estimated one million strong army of scientists working in various laboratories belonging to both private and public sector universities and institutions of whom a few thousands are professors and senior level scientists and the rest are a bulk of junior scientists and doctoral and post doctoral research scientists, who conduct most of their experiments in laboratories. Nearly two thirds of the scientific workforce is employed in research institutions belonging to multinational corporations. Hence it is not surprising that a dominant share of novel technologies and products, patented and entering markets, belong to multinational corporations. More and more research projects and the resulting discoveries are funded by private multinational corporations including the ones taken up by public sector universities in the name of public-private partnerships, are aimed at production of products that could potentially bring profits. For this reason, noble ideas of science such as search for truth, unbranded scientific perusal are eroding and are being replaced by indifference or scientific corruption. It signals the commodification of science.

Knowledge workers (scientists, design engineers and software professionals) also invest a significant portion of social labour in development of technologies, adoption of which helps workers to increase their productivity and production. In fact, they are very much part of the new face of the proletariat.

Modern Science in Service of Capital, Getting Commodified Increasingly

Modern science is a product of capitalism. The economic foundations of modern science were laid in the late 17th century and coincided with the beginning of the Industrial Revolution. Capitalism requires science to expand production, to spread globally, and make production methods more profitable. Science was initially used by capitalism in its fight against feudalism and religious obscurantism. New production technologies based on discoveries in basic science are instantly adopted to expand production and profit margins. Towards the end of the last century scientific production became an essential part of many areas of capitalist production such as electronics, military, aviation, computers and pharmaceutical biotechnology.

Modern industry makes science a productive force distinct from labour and presses it into the service of capital. Technology is an arm and a product of that science. Technology therefore is not neutral. It is employed to increase profits and a weapon of capital pointed at the working class. It has enabled capital to disperse production around the globe and thereby create a genuinely international division of labour. The alienation led to more oppression. Previously workers were closely associated with their machines and tools. This close association with the means of production was chiefly responsible for introduction of new methods and techniques that led to productivity improvement. Introduction of modern technologies at the work place such as automation and robotization of production lines (like the automated auto mobile assembly plants in the Maruti plant) have totally and radically transformed the workplace bringing in revolutionary changes. Automation assembly plants in many factories do not require a worker to invest his or her individual skill or methods to improve production efficiency, but it is also a fact that a worker has either to stand at a spot in the automation assembly line and simply obey the dictated instructions of the computer control system (in a limited time span) or monitoring the computer screens and finally result in 'alienation' of workers themselves. Introduction of new technologies affected both the volume and nature of industrial production, size and composition of the working class, their relation with the means of production, decline in unionization and bargaining power and finally internationalization of production and labour.

Alienation Results in Unemployment, Fall in Wages, Trade Unionism

Decrease in workers' time on factory shop floors led to erosion of employment in the manufacturing sector. This in turn led to swelling of the number of workers in sectors of services such as marketing, distribution, hotel, healthcare and others. Export of capital and distribution of production across the globe (facilitated by modern science and technology) in search of cheap labour and availability of raw materials and resources resulted in increased casualization, neglect of environmental laws, decline in unionization and working class militancy. Technological innovation changed capital's tendency to increase the proportion of dead or constant capital as against the living (that is of workers) or variable capital involved in the production process. In a way capital's attack on workers resulted in decline in collective power, bargaining ability, in the name of austerity, erosion of workers' wages and social wage.

A majority of farmers in millions immigrating from the countryside are not interested in joining the ranks of workers, yet are forced to do so. Millions of farmers are seen on the factory floor (in some cases as casual or contractuals) but as casual wage labourers especially in areas of service industry such as construction, transport and hotels. This fate is being shared by millions of farmers. Fall in wages, rise in casual labourers and refusal to pay insurance, provident fund and other life security benefit measures is the reality of life for workers in the current phase of neoliberalism. Multinational capital is no longer prepared to pay the costs of reproduction of labour as in the past. When they can hire ten casual workers for the salary of one regular worker, why should they bother to regularize them?

New technology and multinational capital also imposed different neoliberal economic policies on sovereign states forcing facilitation of expanded production, exploitation of raw material resources and cheap local labour force.

Introduction of new technology has historical antecedents. In the first quarter of this century the dominant forces within the working class were largely the craftsmen, the highly skilled engineering workers who provided the nucleus of industrial production during the last century. Faced with the threat of success of socialism in several countries and other revolutionary movements and fearful of the spread of their ideas, capital undertook a drastic reshaping of production with the aim of de-skilling the labour force and separating it from its political vanguards.

5

21st Century Perspective for Indian Democracy

C.R. Bakshi

The basic fabric of Indian society, woven in unity with diversity, with multiplicity in language, culture, caste and religion, geographical variations and extremely uneven economic developments with means of production ranging from primitive level to supersonics, is unparalleled in the world.

This uniqueness in Indian society compelled the national leaders to prepare the Constitution of India which is one of the largest among all democracies in the world, in an effort to accommodate in it the interests of all the sections of people, their multiple aspirations and demands and also the dreams cherished during the independence struggle.

Unresolved Contradictions: Dr. Ambedkar's Regret

The bourgeois-democratic members of the Constituent Assembly could not resolve the contradictions in the final draft of the Constitution. The Chairman of the Drafting Committee, Dr. B.R. Ambedkar, while affixing his signature on the final draft, said:

> On the 26th January, 1950, we are going to enter into a life of contradictions. In politics we will have equality and in social and economic life we will have inequality. We must remove

> this contradiction at the earliest possible or else those who suffer from inequality will blow up the structure of political democracy which this Assembly has so laboriously built up.

Thus the basic contradiction of 'inequality' continues to chase Indian democracy and its democratic institutions, to allow the state to help the powerful rich and to neglect the weaker sections in society who are in an overwhelming majority among the people.

Contradiction of Directive Principles and Fundamental Rights

In Our Constitution, originally the 'Right to Property' was included in the 'Fundamental Rights'. Articles 19 and 31 say, "No person shall be deprived of his property save by authority of law." But the Directive Principles of state policy stated in Article 39 that the state shall direct its policy towards securing 39(b) that the ownership and control of the material resources of the community are so distributed as best to sub-serve the common good and 39(c) that the operation of the economic system does not result in the concentration of wealth and means of production to the common detriment.

The directions are clear. But as the Right to Property was initially a fundamental right, the state did not care to honour the above directions to secure the ownership and also the control of the material resources to sub-serve the common good of the community. Neither did the state take any measures to prevent concentration of wealth and means of production.

It was only during the later part of the 1960s, when the left parties had launched movements for nationalization of basic industries like coal mining, oil companies, textiles, banking, insurance, etc. and the ruling Congress Party became weaker due to the split into Syndicate and Indicate, the central government took decisions to secure the ownership and control of some material resources and also nationalized major banks, coal mines, etc. by implementing the decision with full support of the left parties and members of the Indicate in Parliament. Public Sector units were established in a big way in many states. Land reform measures were also taken in hand and the Privy Purse to the erstwhile kings of the estates was abolished. It was really a period of advancement of democracy in the country. But in 1975, promulgation of 'emergency' proved to be counterproductive and anti-democracy, giving a handle to reactionary forces to take advantage and weaken whatever gains were achieved.

When the Supreme Court pronounced the decision in the Keshavananda Bharati case, the Right to Property had been a fundamental right. But in 1978, the 44th amendment to the Constitution deleted the sentence that said, "No person shall be deprived of his property save by authority of law" from the list of fundamental rights and added a new Article 300A with the purpose of making 'right to property' open for the state to deal with specific cases whether compensation was to be given, if a part or whole of a private property was to be acquired by the state.

The present position is that the right to property is not a fundamental right now. But in the Supreme Court, even the government counsels argue in an ambiguous way to safeguard the interests of private owners making the plea of globally liberalized economic policies in favour of private owners under neoliberalism.

However, in 2010, in a Public Interest Litigation (PIL) before the Supreme Court filed by Sanjiv Agrawal, founder of the Kolkata-based Good Governance India Foundation, seeking a direction again to make 'right to property' a Fundamental Right was rejected by the court on the ground that the 42nd Amendment Act 1976 has added in the Preamble of the Constitution the words 'Sovereign Socialist and Secular, it is Parliament which can consider the matter for any change. It was never done.

With the present policy being pursued, Mukesh Ambani alone had wealth of Rs. 1,45,320.08 crores in August 2007 while the 533 billionaires of India including Mukesh Ambani, had their total wealth of Rs. 12,32,135.00 crores that year. By now they must have multiplied their wealth enormously.

In such a state of affairs, why should Parliament not take a clear stand on the issue? Why are the left and democratic parties not demanding to delete Article 300A altogether from the Constitution?

One can understand that silence over this issue means allowing the ruling class, the multinationals, the corporate houses and the handful of corrupt politicians to increase their assets, concentrate wealth and means of production under their ownership making the majority of people deprived of economic rights and equality. This is going against democracy and corrupting society. India is now suffering from such a degeneration that even our cultural ethos has degenerated to dishonour the women in society whom we worship adoring: '*Janani Janmabhumishcha Swargadapi Gariyasi.*'

Is Parliament in Total Disarray?

Really, our Parliament appears to be in total disarray, as Lenin once described the character of a bourgeois parliament. So many criminals have entered Parliament as so-called people's representatives. Some of them are billionaires by amassing money and property through the pillage of national wealth. With nearly 300 millionaires, it has become almost a super rich people's club where more than 160 persons have criminal charges. As reported, there are 162 MPs in the Lok Sabha who have more than 522 criminal cases against them, 14 of murders, 20 attempts to murder, 11 of duping people and 13 of kidnappings. It is a shame to the nation that in our 'highest temple of democracy' the cases of 'cash for question,' 'money to buy MPs', 'porn films' and such other disgraceful acts are reported. All these are the consequences of neoliberal economic policies which have been adopted by the country since 1990-91.

They say the 'Taj Mahal' of 21st century India stands there in Mumbai with the name 'Antilia' as an achievement of Indian democracy. It is a personal property of Mukesh Ambani, on a plot of 48,780 sq.ft. with its land price of 11 crore 40 lakh rupees and total value of not less than Rs. 2,500 crore. The author of a book *Ambani Sons*, has described Mukesh Ambani as 'the new Maharaja of India'. Ratan Tata however said, "Antilia is an example of a rich Indian's lack of empathy for the poor". Some Indians are proud of the 'Ostentatious house' of Mukesh Ambani. Of course, some others say, "shameful in a nation where many children go hungry". But there was no criticism made in Parliament except by one or two left MPs.

It is amusing to note that designed by American architects with 27 floors of the structure called 'Antilia', has no two floor plans alike and there is a total of 4,000 sq. ft. of living space for only six members of the Ambani family. The palace has space for 168 cars for parking with one floor exclusively for maintenance of the vehicles, nine elevators in the lobby, three helicopter pads, three floors with hanging gardens and ball room including an ice-room for playing with ice.

One cannot and must not agree with such a democracy to be rich where rich and corrupt rule the roost.

Search for Alternatives

No election with the present political system will change the fate of the country. No legislation of Lok Pal or Jan Lok Pal will be able to eradicate corruption. No Anna Hazare or Kejriwal with their crusade against corruption will succeed unless the socio-economic inequality and gap between the rich and poor is reduced to a rational level. The newly emerged Aam Admi Party has chosen the broom (*jhadu*) as an election symbol to clean the floor to 'democracy'. This reminds me of a story in the Bengali Poem 'Juta Avishkar' (Discovery of a Shoe) written by Rabindranath Tagore.

Once a King named Habu Roy asked his minister Gobu Roy to clean the dust on earth which soiled his feet. He chided, "Your people take a salary but do not look after my inconveniences; remove the dust on earth, else I will punish you". Heads of the wise men rolled, seventeen and a half lakh *jhadus* were bought to sweep the dust. But in the process dust rose towards the sky as clouds to cover the sun and the earth. Then 21 lakhs of watermen were engaged to spread water on the dust. That emptied the ponds and rivers to make the fish and the people suffer and die. Again the wise men met and planned to keep the king in prison so as not to let him touch the dust. That too failed. Then came an old cobbler with a piece of leather to cover the feet of the king and the king was saved from the dust. The '**shoe**' came into use since then. The ministers and others also got a new life.

A simile can be drawn linking this story with the preaching and practice by the Aam Adami Party engaged in sweeping work everywhere in the country in the name of ending corruption. They will fail in their campaign if these actions remain within the limits of 'anarchism' as Kejriwal himself named it. They are to perfect themselves and make their ideology equipped with the knowledge and world experience of genuine democratic practices based on science.

Alternative Path for Genuine Democracy

Finally, turning back to Dr. Ambedkar over the problem of 'contradiction' in the Constitution of India, the pamphlet written by V.I. Lenin called 'The Proletarian Revolution and the Renegade Kautsky' has a relevance in the Indian situation. Lenin writes:

> The more highly democracy is developed, the more the bourgeois parliaments are subjected by the stock exchange and the bankers. Even in the most democratic bourgeois state the oppressed people at every step encounter the crying contradictions between the formal equality proclaimed by the 'democracy' of the capitalists and the thousands of real limitations and subterfuges which turn the proletariats into wage slaves. It is precisely this contradiction that is opening the eyes of the people to the rotten mediocrity and hypocrisy of capitalism. It is this contradiction that the agitators and propagandists of socialism are constantly exposing to the people, in order to prepare them for revolution. (*Selected Works*, Vol. 3, 1977, pp. 31 and 37)

This is what is exactly necessary to be done in India today—prepare for a genuine democratic revolution, through agitations, propaganda and exposure of capitalist loot of resources and wealth of the nation. All the left parties with their ideology of socialism should join hands with those democrats who are committed to 'sovereignty, socialism and secularism', the goal of Indian democracy as has been solemnly resolved, to build a strong joint movement for necessary amendments in the Constitution, to implement the Directive Principles of State Policy in letter and spirit.

The parties subscribing to the views of neoliberalism and fundamentalism to help capitalist exploitation to continue dividing the people of India on religious and communal basis, must be isolated from the masses, particularly the younger generation. In that the left parties with firm ideology as well as flexibility in approach, have a pioneering role to play in the 21st century.

6

On the Verge of a Shift That Never Was

Krishna Jha

The time has come to analyse and formulate, though hardly available, the tools, the concepts that could adequately focus on the issues that challenge the hitherto existing, though fast getting obsolete, ways of understanding. There is not only a total shift in the tenets of historical materialism, but also a crisis in philosophy. However, the turns that are appearing have not been unexpected, only the dimensions remained unknown.

It was Karl Marx who had as early as in the late 1850s, foreseen the evolution of machines towards automation and that in the process would substitute human labour and thus would change the organic composition of capital. In this context comes primarily the labour theory of value, the contract of labour with the capitalist where the worker gives more and gets less in return, generating surplus, which is the core contradiction of capitalism.

Marx was aware that the process of production would reach a point where labour would become superfluous. He wrote in *Grundrisse: Introduction to the Critique of Political Economy*, '... Labour no longer appears so much to be included in the production process, rather the human being comes to relate more as a watchman or regulator to the production process itself... (The worker) then steps to the side of the production process, instead of being its chief actor.' But even before that, in the final para 'On Commodity', (*Capital,* Vol. 1), he had indicated the stage when time and space would disappear and motion would be the only reality.

He wrote further, '...In this transformation, it is neither the direct human labour he himself performs, nor the time during which he works, but rather the appropriation of his own general productive power, his understanding of nature, and his mastery over it by virtue of his presence as a social body—it is, in a word, the development of the social individual, which appears as the great foundation stone of production and social wealth. The theft of alien labour time, on which the present wealth is based, appears as a miserable foundation in face of this new one, created by large scale industry. As soon as labour in the direct form has ceased to be the great well spring of wealth, labour time ceases, and must cease to be its measure, and hence, exchange value, use value..'

Here comes the end of exploitation in the classical sense, and also alienation. In the process of capitalist development, emerges the social individual, harbinger of the new society. The substitution of science for labour as the chief force of production is inevitable as Marx pointed out, capital calls to life all the powers of science and nature ... in order to make creation of wealth independent (relatively) of the labour time employed in it.

Marx had visualized the transformations, living in the machine age, unleashed by the steam engine along with a few scientific discoveries.

Today, the class divided socio-economic formations that evolved with the shifts in basis and superstructure, have become witness to science becoming the direct force of production. Also a need has emerged to forge an alliance of new progressive forces in the struggle for freedom today. The new society to be created thus would have to be based on a new concept of democracy, since there are unprecedented changes in the social composition itself. None of the issues can be taken up unless in the context of the scientific and technological as well as information and communication revolution (STR and ICR).

Though the challenges are yet to be interpreted, it is true that the democratic revolution in this era has to be different from the industrial era of the 20th century. While tracing the evolution of the concept of the democratic revolution, along with Lenin, who had conceptualized it early in 1905, when he wrote the *Two Tactics of Social Democracy,* among other eminent philosophers is the name of Italian revolutionary Antonio Gramsci. Lenin had categorized the process of transition to socialism as to go through different stages completing anti-feudal and anti-imperialist tasks. It was a step ahead in Marxist theory, in which Marx and Engels had stressed the democratic rights and institutions. They also advocated the use of parliamentary and democratic forms and institutions after fighting for them and wanted a peaceful transition to socialism.

According to Antonio Gramsci (1891-1937), known as a theoretician of superstructure, the revolutionary movement should start with everyday life of the working class that is in other words, he stressed the notion of totality. He also believed in the importance of ideological struggle in the process of socialist transformation. He had tried to forge alliances with sections of peasantry and wanted it to serve as the social basis for the workers' state. He was a prominent labour leader, was in Moscow and Vienna working for the Comintern and finally in 1926, was arrested by the fascist regime in Italy and died in extremely unhealthy conditions in 1937, after serving ten years in prison where he wrote his famous *Prison Notebooks*. In his notes, he focused on the role of intellectuals, about whom he said, 'All men are intellectuals... but not all men in the society have the function of intellectuals.' He said that each social class, creates together with itself, organically, one or more strata of intellectuals which give it homogeneity, and an awareness of the new function not only in economic but also in the social and political fields. Gramsci categorized the intellectuals as organic and traditional, and among them the traditional intellectuals considered themselves independent of the social classes existing in that particular period. They bore a historical continuity above and beyond socio-political changes, like philosophers and writers. These intellectuals are actually survivors of the past, since they were parts of the superstructure in which the base, the particular mode of production is already obsolete, hence far from reality, their ideology was idealist. The organic intellectuals were those who were directly related to the classes they belonged to. They reflected the collective consciousness of the class in the political, economic and social spheres. However these organic intellectuals were also autonomous and enjoyed a certain degree of freedom from the class they belonged to.

Among the functions of the intellectuals identified by Gramsci was to preserve the hegemony of their class over the society as a whole with a justifying ideology which they represented. Both the concepts of intellectuals and hegemony were contributions of Gramsci to Marxist theory. These concepts were not new but were used till now in a narrow sense by the Comintern in its documents and also by Plekhanov.

Dealing with superstructure, Gramsci discusses the concept of civil society, that is a combination of organizations commonly called private, meaning also political. He also stresses that the ways adopted by civil society of establishing and organizing human relationships are deeply political and should be taken as integral to class domination. Also according to Gramsci, civil society corresponds to hegemony, or direct domination or command.

So far as forms of control are concerned, social hegemony indicates spontaneous consent, given by the masses to the general direction imposed on social life by the dominant fundamental group (meaning the ruling class or bourgeoisie). This consent is historically caused by the superior position enjoyed by the dominant group or the confidence that consequently comes, in its position and function in the world of production.

In the process of control also comes the apparatus of state coercive power wielded by the political government to legally enforce discipline on those who refuse to consent either actively or passively. However, such force is hardly used as he wrote, 'the intellectuals of the historically progressive class, in the given conditions, exercise such a power of attraction that in the last analysis they end up by subjugating the intellectuals of the other social groups, ... thereby create a system of solidarity between all the intellectuals ...' He said that the world view of the ruling class was so thoroughly diffused by its intellectuals as to become the common sense of the whole society. In fact most of the time, the ruling class had no use for force to exert its dominance. Gramsci said that when the ruling class does not have ideological hegemony over the masses, it even steals its intellectuals, adding that 'If you see the whole history of Italy up to the present time, you can see that a small group of leaders methodically succeeded in absorbing into itself the political personnel thrown up by the movements of the masses that were subversive in origin...' Gramsci had the experience of the Second International too where the working class movements failed to resist the 'bourgeois ideological hegemony.'

To exercise hegemony in the parliamentary system of democracy, there is stress on consent and there is also an attempt to ensure that force is made to appear as if coming with consent from the majority that gets expression in the organs of public opinion, that is media, and such public opinion is artificially multiplied. In such a situation, the contradictory nature of capitalism is never exposed since their ideological hegemony is exercised as representing the interest of the society as a whole. There are compromises also made in the process to keep the allies that consent and get unified in a social bloc of forces. Gramsci called this the historical bloc, that represents a social order, in which the hegemony of the ruling class is created and recreated in a web of institutions, social relations and ideas. This 'fabric of hegemony' is woven by intellectuals who have an organized role in society. Thus, Gramsci goes beyond the definition of the state as the instrument of a class. He employs the concept of hegemony to argue that any economic notion of politics or ideology which looks for an immediate economic class interest in politics and culture is incapable of an accurate analysis of the political situation and of the balance of political forces and cannot produce an adequate understanding of the nature of state power (economism). Consequently it is also inadequate as a basis for political strategy for the working class movement.

Gramsci believed that to establish its own hegemony, the working class has to come out of its own sectarian narrow interests, and assert to ensure the interest of society as a whole. It may be pointed out here that Gramsci was working in the Communist International in the post October Revolution days when Lenin had forwarded the theory of the first anti-feudal bourgeois democratic revolution with the broadest possible alliances, and even handed over the power in February 1917 to the Mensheviks. Later as

Bolsheviks assumed the state power, Lenin called it dictatorship of the proletariat and the poor peasantry, an alliance for which Gramsci said that the working class had surrendered its economic interest to an extent. But by 1922-23, it started getting clearer that the basic character of the state power was unchanged. It had undergone a change 'only on its surface,' wrote Lenin, and again warned against any assumption that there were enough elements for the building of a really new state apparatus. Hence once again, Lenin's formulation that in the era of imperialism, transition to socialism has to undergo various democratic stages, accomplishing anti-feudal, anti-imperialist tasks with broadest possible alliance with forces opposed to imperialist vested interest was vindicated. It was also at this stage that Lenin attacked the thesis forwarded by M.N. Roy, an Indian revolutionary in the Comintern who along with many others was opposed to any alliance, adjustment or cooperation with the bourgeois forces despite their anti-imperialist stance. Lenin was of the firm opinion that especially in the under developed countries like India, the united anti-colonial democratic front was the only way out. The concept of the broad alliance uniting the democratic forces in a front was again brought to focus by Georgy Dimitrov when he fought against the sectarian tendencies in the Comintern in 1935, two years before Gramsci died in a fascist prison, a tragedy that could have been averted if the Dimitrov thesis had its way. The broad bourgeois democratic alliance advanced by Lenin, blossomed in the Dimitrov thesis, which if implemented could have stalled Nazism as well as fascism. This period was identified as a phase of popular fronts, especially in Europe, but so far as the countries of east Europe were concerned, in the years just before the Second World War, there were people's democratic fronts organized to face the onslaught of fascism. In Asia, China was one example of how to form the people's united front, since the Chinese Communist Party had even formed an anti-imperialist front with the Kuomintang, that under the leadership of Chiang Kai-shek had ruthlessly fought the communists. However, in the aftermath of the Second World War, the spectrum of democracy got widened as never before. There was a distinct shift in the forces and a possibility of social change emerged, where the concept of the people's democratic front could not be applied. The struggle for democratic rights became widespread as never before, with grounds for peaceful means of change, defeat of imperialism, completion of the process of democratic revolution and finally the clarity in the concept of national democracy. It was descending on the popular consciousness that a front with a broad and flexible cooperation was needed and was possible with the forces of all anti-imperialist and democratic forces, combining national and also class interest dialectically.

Gramsci, in his *Prison Notebooks*, observed that the fight against the ideological hegemony of the capitalist class was imperative, and for that has to be forged the broadest alliances surrendering narrow interests, and sometimes even making compromises, offering a counter culture representing larger sections of civil society, which could later serve as the social base for the working class. It was only then that ascendancy to state power could be imagined.

Gramsci was primarily waging the struggle against fascism that had seized Italy and was looming over entire Europe. More than a hundred years have elapsed. Concepts and formations keep evolving. The concept of democracy is no more applicable in the same way. The leading socialist system has collapsed. And most importantly, science is fast becoming a substitute for human labour. Action-oriented skills are no longer required for immediate knowledge. The age of assembly workers with their hands directly on the raw material in the process of production is gone. There is a growing need to get the connection between the symbol and reality closer, since labour means cognitive activity to interpret symbols. In the context of an emerging new era, institutions are coming up to assert a new type of democracy. Masses are equipped with new means of knowledge where the surroundings are shrinking and also expanding. The role of science has been changing. Right to knowledge is no more restricted to only a few, it has been getting democratized.

The ideological balance has been shifting with new turns in practical and theoretical stages. As Gramsci had observed, the working class has to win over the minds of people. In a socio-economic formation, where definition of labour has been undergoing a historical change, it is possible in the process of struggle itself to achieve hegemony of democratic ideas forging alliances with the broadest possible forces and isolating the imperialist capitalist forces.

Vietnam has been the guiding example for forming a united front. It had fought for more than a century against the colonial/imperialist onslaught and yet had its own consolidation of forces. The entire nation fought as one. The countries with immense resources committed aggression against this small and brave nation for decades, yet all of them were kept isolated. The identity of Vietnam remained intact as also its will to create a socialist system.

In many of the Latin American countries, there are broad alliances with social and political forces Mass media has become a source of strength catering to the vast masses and giving rise to the information revolution.

The issue that arises here is no more concerned with the working class in a classical sense, since the base itself has undergone transformation, and that brings forth the need to redefine the concepts of democracy as well as socialism.

Democracy and the democratic institutions have been blossoming not only at the national level but also across the borders of the nations, at the international level. In the entire process, the role of STR is gaining significance as are arising new theoretical discourses, since it is increasingly getting difficult to define the socio-economic formations in terms of base and superstructure.

7

Democracy and Socialism: The Indian Scenario

M. Aravind Kumar

"The first step in the revolution by the working class is to raise the proletariat to the position of ruling class to win the battle of democracy."

Karl Marx and Frederick Engels in
The Communist Manifesto, Chapter 2

The politics of Marx and Engels would be incomplete if it is not understood in terms of their relationship to democracy both as a theory and as a movement. Marx and Engels never spoke against democracy as such. Rather they were staunch opponents of liberal or bourgeois democracy and stressed the need for a socialist democracy. If democracy refers to a 'rule of the people' then whom does the word 'people' refer to, whether it refers to the exploiting classes like capitalists, landlords or the exploited ones like workers, toilers, or in simple terms 'working masses'? For Marx and Engels it included only the 'working masses', and it is thus that the meaning and operation of democracy must change with the changing nature of the word 'people'.

Marx and Engels were critical of bourgeois democracy, not because it was democratic, but because it was bourgeois, and they proposed to effect their critique in practice by using the space provided by bourgeois democracy for the achievement of socialist democracy. Thus in their view the basic and primary requirement of a democratic system is to give power to the workers and peasants who will in turn liquidate all the exploiters and oppressors. Thus the condition precedent for the advent of a democratic system is the existence of a classless society.

Democracy thereby becomes a proletarian principle, a principle of the masses. It is with this in view that we should understand democracy and democratic revolutions in any country. In India too we have a rich legacy of democratic movements right through the 20th century.

The struggle for working class or proletarian democracy would be incomplete without completing the tasks which a bourgeois democratic revolution requires. For achieving this objective, a progressive and democratic programme for accomplishment of immediate tasks which a socialist revolution requires becomes vital. An assessment of the past and present accomplishments would be of great help in charting out a programme for a successful socialist revolution in our country.

Socialism in India

History shows that in the course of historical development each country has passed through various stages. In a particular stage of development it could be witnessed that apart from the major classes there always existed various other classes of people. For example, in a slave society apart from the slave owners and slaves there existed independent people, artisans, craftsmen, etc. Similarly in the case of feudal society, where the major antagonistic classes were the feudal lords and serfs one could find independent small scale producers, craftsmen, traders, etc. This situation could be witnessed under capitalism also where we could witness the existence of monopoly capitalists, along with whom there are middle classes, petty bourgeoisie, mental labourers, from scientists to office workers, etc apart from the mainstream capitalists and the proletariat.

In a similar fashion the Indian situation resembles the conditions of countries developing under a capitalistic path of social development. It is a fact that the birth of the Indian proletariat preceded that of the Indian capitalists. The railways, mines and tea estates were brought in by the British rulers. They changed the village economic system of India by merging it with the British market. The merchants and intermediaries within India gradually grew up as Indian capitalists at a later stage. During the First and Second World Wars the British government due to the opposition they faced and to further their war requirements were obliged to allow the growth of the Indian capitalists.

Organization of the Indian Bourgeoisie

Though the Indian working class was born even before the birth of Indian capitalism, it never had any proper working class organization till the formation of the All India Trade Union Congress (AITUC) of 1920. However even before that class conscious Indian bourgeoisie had founded its own organization in 1885, and it was the Indian National Congress. The Indian bourgeoisie demanded an independent development without any barriers created by imperialism. Naturally they evinced interest in opposing the British rule in a manner which was appealing to the people. However they never hesitated to give up the struggle whenever the people's movement crossed the threshold level. They were keen to retain their leadership in the freedom struggle. Sometimes when the workers' and peasants' movement became very intense they were prepared to make concessions to the British. However it should be borne in mind that though they made concessions to the British at times their general class character was anti-imperialist and always remained proponents of an independent path of development.

In fact from 1920, AITUC functioned as an organization for the united front comprising wide sections of the masses. It also sought to establish an organization on the agricultural front. But the Kanpur Conspiracy case of 1924 presented an obstacle in accomplishing this task.

However efforts were made to unite all the splinter communist groups in various parts of the country. Thus the CPI was established as an all India party of the working class and peasants. Following this various mass organizations were founded. The workers' struggle took place in key industrial centres like Bombay and Calcutta. Foundations were laid in Punjab and Uttar Pradesh for building the Kisan movement. The communists gave the call for independence all over the country. They also worked in the Congress as its members for fulfilling the primary task of achieving independence before venturing to build socialism.

From 1925 to 1929 the communist movement discharged its national task in an efficient manner. During this period within the Congress two different trends emerged. One group preferred some sort of bargaining and achieving reforms within the British rule, while the other one demanded *Poorna Swaraj* (complete independence) and stood for conducting mass struggles.

From that point of time the communists started supporting the radical and progressive section within the Congress against the reactionary group. This tactic was adopted after the path laid down by Comrade Lenin in the second congress of the Third International. Accordingly it was emphasized that the task of the communists in the colonial nations was to conduct an intense struggle against imperialism. At the same time they should render support to the leftist sections within the bourgeoisie against those trying to make peace with imperialism. The communists while working inside the Congress had their own platform for building the party of workers and peasants. The major aspects of CPI's tactics during this period were the following:

- Working in unity within the national framework along with the bourgeoisie.
- Fighting against the compromising sections within the Congress.
- Radicalizing the left wing within the Congress.
- Rendering the support of workers and peasants for the left wing.
- Carrying forward progressive slogans to the people by an independent and separate organization.
- Conducting class struggles by establishing Workers – Peasants Organizations.

These tactics yielded great results as very soon after its birth the Communist Party of India grew in a rapid manner and became an unavoidable force in the national movement. Thus the communists due to the right kind of tactics were able to carry out both their national and class tasks in an efficient manner.

The Sectarian Path and National Front

The British government was alarmed at the rising 'Bolshevik threat'. It yielded to the voices of the Association of the British Capitalists and it ended with the 'Meerut Conspiracy case' of 1929. This case was imposed with a view to sideline the communists from the national stream. Many comrades were arrested and imprisoned. At this juncture came the decisions of the Sixth Conference of the Third International. This was received by the comrades who were working outside and finally the leadership outside made changes which was entirely contradictory to its current successful path. Accordingly the national struggle under Gandhi's leadership was known as 'Reformism' and it was proposed that a separate front of the working class should be formed by isolating itself from the reformist elements. This path was in reality a left sectarian one. It failed to see the anti-imperialist character of the national bourgeoisie. This in turn made the situation favourable for the British rulers. Oppressions became intense against the party organizations and at a point of time the party became entirely isolated from the masses in the freedom struggle.

This trend continued till 1934 and finally the Meerut prisoners were released. Efforts were made to correct the sectarian path which was being pursued then. The guidelines and advice by the Seventh Congress and along with it the Dutt-Bradley thesis propounded by the Communist Party of Great Britain helped to correct the mistakes committed by the party in India. The wrong guidelines of the sixth Congress were reversed. The necessity of a National Front came to the fore.

Thus by 1937, the CPI came to a correct position regarding the class character of the national bourgeoisie. Once again it witnessed a tremendous growth among wide sections of the people in India. Similarly under the fascist threat during the Second World War, Comrade Dimitrov put forward his thesis in the seventh Congress of the Third International. He emphasized the need for the communists to work in the United Front against the fascist forces. This was implemented successfully in the countries of Europe where both the national bourgeoisie and the working classes fought together against fascism.

However in India conditions were of a different kind where the national bourgeoisie wanted to overthrow the imperialist rule immediately during the war but the communists were bound to hold back their struggles against the British for the moment after the USSR joined the allies in the struggle against the fascist forces. Thus the communists were bound to uphold their proletarian internationalism for which they were criticized by the national bourgeoisie as betrayers of the freedom movement. In any case this line was ended immediately after the war and once again mass struggles continued against imperialism in India. Heroic struggles like the revolt of the Royal Indian Navy and mass level strikes and agitations by the workers and peasants were supported by the party which in turn pressurized the British to grant independence to India.

Finally India became independent in 1947.

Post Independence Era

If we glance briefly at the history of socialism in India we can comprehend that one major obstacle for the growth of the communist party is the wrong assessment of the national bourgeoisie which was repeated very often at several junctures. This continued even after the struggle for independence which was the cause of the adventurist and self-destructive path taken by the party in 1948. The assessment by the communists of the situation at that time was that the bourgeois leadership had betrayed the people to imperialism and feudalism. The suppression of the struggles of 1947-48, especially the Telangana struggle on the one hand, and the rampant spread of communal violence on the other hand, provoked the communists to rise against the state. They held that the national bourgeoisie that had betrayed the revolution should be ousted from power by intensifying the class struggle and finally a people's democratic state should be established under the leadership of the proletariat. This in turn resulted in grave consequences for the party and its mass organizations. In other words, the Communist Party failed to view the national task facing it and rather gave undue importance to the class task.

The Phase of Transition

The call for the establishment of people's democracy received an unwelcome response from the people in India. Rather it gave an opportunity for the bourgeoisie to express their repressions against the party and its cadres. The entire party apparatus was smashed to a considerable level.

During that period with a view to correct the line taken by the party from 1948-50, the Chinese leadership under Chairman Mao Tse tung stressed the importance of uniting with the national bourgeoisie to take part in the building of the new republic. However his advice was rejected by the then leadership of CPI under Comrade B.T. Ranadive.

It is important to take note of the path taken by the Communist Party of China [CPC] till the formation of the People's Republic of China in 1949 and also till the eighth Congress of the CPC in 1956. It is also vital to have a grasp of the concept of 'New Democracy' propounded by Chairman Mao. The most important document in this regard would be 'The Two Tactics of the Social Democratic Revolution' by Comrade Lenin. The crux of this work is that during the period of the bourgeois democratic revolution, communists should lead the struggles of the workers and peasants and should play a pivotal role in completing the anti-imperialist and anti-feudal revolution. For accomplishing this task a broad democratic front should be created based on the unity of workers and peasants and including the national bourgeoisie within the front. And within the front the tactics of unity and struggle should be followed in dealing with the national bourgeoisie. Through these tactics the imperialist and feudal elements will be isolated and at the same time the national bourgeoisie will also be fought against when it comes to the welfare of workers and peasants.

It is not wrong to say that the assessment made by Comrade Ranadive in that period was that both the bourgeois democratic revolution and socialist revolution have merged together, and also that the Indian state was headed by the big bourgeoisie in alliance with feudalism and imperialism.

Hence a proposal was made to capture the cities through the armed insurrection of the workers and establish people's democracy. It was a replication of the Russian path. However later during the 1960's along with the comrades who went out of the party gave a call once again for the capture of the state machinery but this time following the model of the Chinese path.

This is the irony of history.

Neither the Russian path nor the Chinese path could help in establishing socialism in India.

Rather the answer for the question of the Socialist revolution in our country is an Indian path fulfilling both its national task and class tasks simultaneously. Thus sectarianism and adventurism had always been an impediment for the progress and growth of the party. The split inside the communist movement in 1964 and creation of CPI(M), leaving the mother party of the CPI, and then further split in the CPI(M) in 1969 which led to the Naxalite movement and various other splinter groups have in turn weakened the position of the Left inside the country.

National Democracy

In the initial stage after the revolution, Comrade Lenin had put forward the 'New Economic Policy'. It was in reality an economic preparation for a full-fledged socialist revolution. This policy shows the way a country with an economic system with multiple heads should follow. Comrade Lenin had explained this further in his historic essays like 'April Thesis', 'The Immediate Tasks of the Working Class', 'Tax in Kind', etc. where he presented the complete picture of Russia at that time. He explains the multi-headed economic system of Russia and the measures to be taken for consolidation of socialism.

National democracy when compared with people's democracy provided us with more avenues for growth and development of the working class in India and the Third World. The economic framework of the Indian state at that time cannot be called a full-fledged capitalist set up as such. But rather it could be termed as a capitalist dominated system with multiple heads. Though industrial capitalism held the mantle of economic growth it was not the entire contributor in the economic system of India. Rather we can say that agriculture was the major factor in the economic growth along with small and medium-scale industries. This situation though not entirely but to some extent resembled Russia during the revolution of 1917. A few months after the revolution there existed a nationalized public sector, private sector, small-scale production, rich peasants and peasants with small holdings.

Towards a Broader and New Kind of Democracy

Both national and people's democracies had the same objective, that is fulfilment of the tasks of the bourgeois democratic revolution and to lay the basis for a socialist democratic revolution. They are against imperialism, feudalism and monopoly. As far as the duties are concerned, both have the same view that is eradication of the hold of foreign capital, abolishing the remnants of feudalism through radical agrarian reforms, strengthening and defending the public sector, providing support to the national bourgeoisie and at the same time prevent them from growing into big bourgeoisie and thereby ensuring democracy in all spheres of the governance in society. Likewise, if we take into consideration the class composition they are similar, that is participation of the intelligentsia, rich peasants and national bourgeoisie on the basis of the worker-peasant alliance in the rule of the state and in wielding state power. However, the crucial difference lies in the question of 'Who will lead the state?'

Thus under a people's democracy the working class will be in the leading position with others participating as junior partners. On the contrary under a national democracy both the national bourgeoisie and the working class will be equal partners in the wielding of state power. A question may arise as to why this kind of arrangement? Is it because the Communist Party does not want to lead the alliance? Or is it because it has become tail holders of the bourgeoisie through sheer reformism? Why does a people's democracy retain the national bourgeoisie as its junior partner in the alliance? Before one ventures to answer these questions he/she should answer first as to why does the Communist Party whose ultimate aim is communism keep a people's democratic system or a national democratic system as its immediate objective? The answer for these questions could be put this way that all such democratic systems are not the whims and fancies of the communists but they are the resultants of the assessments made taking into consideration the objective and subjective circumstances that are prevalent in society at a particular period of history.

If one claims that we could dispense with all such formulations and directly establish socialism before passing through these phases of history then it would be considered rather a subjective answer to the question of a socialist/ communist revolution. These issues have been dealt with in detail by Comrade Lenin in his 'Left Wing Communism—An Infantile Disorder'. History shows that the world communist movement has suffered very often by the frequent bouts of sectarianism and adventurism. In other cases reformism and revisionism have also played their part to an extent. All these deviations have proved as obstacles and barriers in the progress of socialism and democracy.

In the people's democracies of Europe and other parts of the world established after the Second World War the big bourgeoisie had either collaborated with imperialism as in the case of China or it had betrayed the working class and peasants during the invasion of fascist forces.

Thus naturally the working class and peasants fought against imperialism and fascism and have established a people's democratic state under the head of the working class. In India, the case was different both during the independence struggle and after. The bourgeoisie though it came to a compromise with imperialism in a few instances, their class character was basically an anti- imperialist one.

The Indian economy though dominated by the bourgeoisie was indeed an economic system with multiple heads. A major portion of the income came from the agriculture sector. In the industrial sector the key industries were in the hands of the state. It was not industrial capitalism that headed the economy during the early years after the independence of our country. These were the objective conditions that necessitated the adoption of a national democratic programme. People's democracy at that instant was not a relevant option. This is because of the fact that by proclaiming the leadership of the working class or by forcing the other classes to accept the leadership of the proletariat or by usage of force to weaken the strength of the national bourgeoisie was not a viable option for the establishment of the working class leadership over the Indian state.

Also whenever steps were taken to establish working class rule through armed insurrection and use of force, the left movement in toto was isolated from the mainstream politics and suffered from various splits which diluted the revolutionary fervour and confidence among the masses.

Thus only by building a broad democratic front comprising of possible allies against neoliberalism, feudalism, monopoly and big bourgeoisie through peaceful methods would be the relevant method under Indian circumstances. Also by the end of the 20th century the socialist regimes and people's democracies except for a few have been ousted from power in countries of Europe and various parts of the world. Undoubtedly they came to power with the support of other members in the people's democratic alliance. But history shows that wielding of state power by the working class party through force and by harsh suppression of voices of dissent within these people's democracies made them unpopular among a major section of the people.

The world has changed considerably since the collapse of the socialist regimes in the USSR and other socialist countries. STR and ICR have brought rapid changes in the composition of the working class in the present society. There is an unprecedented and rapid growth of productive forces.

Also it should be kept in mind that there is an acute change in our earlier formulations regarding national democracy. A considerable section of the national bourgeoisie themselves have grown into big bourgeoisie. They have joined the band of big MNCs and giant corporations. Thus a crucial change has taken place in the composition of the national bourgeoisie. Our allies could be native, indigenous and small-scale producers who play an active role in the democratization of the market. Hence the objective of the communists at the present moment would be to broaden and widen the programme of national democracy which would assimilate the growth of productive forces and ensure the participation of various sections of society. The success of a democratic revolution in its real terms lies in the fulfilment of this objective.

8

Discourses of Secularism in India

Rajan Kumar

Rather than abstract theorization, I begin with identifying some of the basic features of discourses of secularism in India over the last two hundred years. What I want to do is to explain the way the Indian state has negotiated with religion at various stages and how this concept was contested at every stage.

Secularism cannot be understood as a fixed or static concept. It refers to a field of differentiated and competitive positions taken by the modern nation-state in its negotiations with religions. It is a dynamic political stance with four underlying assumptions: a) Privileging the role of the state over religious organizations in non-religious activities. b) Recognition of the religious rights of communities. c) Recognition of citizenship rights, and d) Constant negotiation of the state with religion.

If we accept these characteristics, there cannot be a fixed meaning of secularism—it is contextual and evolving. Therefore, to synonymize the entire Western secularism with a singular meaning of 'separation of state with the church' is as misleading as equating Indian secularism with the Western one. This is ahistorical and a non-sequitur. These generalizations subsume the multiplicity of discourses which existed at different historical periods.

Historians have identified three distinct stages in the evolution of secularism in modern India. First is the 'non-interventionist secularism' of the colonial period; second, 'contested secularisms' of the Indian National Movement; and finally, the 'crisis of secularism' in the contemporary times. But if we go further back to the medieval times, the Mughal state had evolved its own mechanisms of dealing with contemporary religions. Ambar's '*Din-e-ilahi*' of Akbar was an eclectic device to encourage a dialogue among various religions and evolve a consensus on conflicting issues. It was an attempt by the state to understand the fundamental assumptions of all religions and encourage religious interaction through a dialogic interaction of various faiths. The three dimensional interactions of religion to religion and religion to state was a novel experiment of that time, something that the modern state is yet to learn.

Colonial Secularism: Selective Intervention

The British followed, by and large, a policy of non-interference or selective interference in religious matters[1]. Since 1858, uniformity in many of the civil and criminal laws was established. But personal laws continued to be governed by religious laws. Colonial rulers did not want to intervene in religious matters which could foment trouble and protest. Colonial rulers intervened only when required by the social reformers and the people. Colonial rule did intervene in some of the social issues with religious overtones such as the Banning of Sati Act, Human Sacrifice Banning Act and so on[2]. But they were either in response to indigenous demands or isolated at best. Indian nationalist leaders criticized and protested against colonial intervention in the cultural identity of the nation. Partha Chatterjee calls it a shift in the agency of reform from the legal authority of the colonial state to the moral authority of the national community[3]. According to him, legal intervention in the cause of religious reform was not undesirable per se, but it was undesirable when the state was colonial.

Constituent Assembly Debates on Secularism

The Constituent Assembly debates reflect the views of nationalist leaders on the issue of secularism. Nehruvian liberalism contested with the Gandhian tolerance while both were disputed by the right-leaning parties, such as, the Muslim League and the Hindu Mahasabha. In this section, we will reflect on three significant issues of the Uniform Civil Code, minority and minority institutions[4]. The drafts of K.M. Munshi and Ambedkar referred indirectly to the virtues of the Uniform Civil Code in a diversified state but the Fundamental Rights sub-committee placed it in the Directive Principles of State Policies. However, there were other leaders such as, Hansa Mehta, Minoo Masani and Amrit Kaur who strongly advocated the Uniform Civil Code. But Mohamed Ismail Saheb and B. Pocker opposed it[5]. Finally, it was concluded that the time was not ripe for implementation at that stage, and hence, it was included in the Directive Principles of State Policies.

On the issue of minority, Ambedkar argued that social discrimination constituted the real test for determining whether a social group is or is not a minority. Thus, both scheduled castes and certain religious groups should be considered a minority. Ambedkar critically questioned Indian nationalism which, according to him, had developed the divine right of the majority to rule over the minority. Any claim for the sharing of power by the minority is called communalism while monopolizing of the whole power by the majority is called nationalism[6].

The issue of minority institutions was also contested fiercely. M. Masani and K.T. Shah advocated the right to religious freedom but opposed the provision of minority religious institutions[7]. While Jayaprakash Narayan argued that cultural and education rights should be permitted to linguistic minorities only, Rajkumari Amrit Kaur rejected the idea of setting up educational institutions by religious minorities. Finally, all minorities, whether based on religion or language were granted the right to establish and administer educational institutions.

Hence, we see that there was hardly any consensus on the nature of secularism and its institutionalization in state practices. The disagreements have had far-reaching implications and Indian politics is still grappling with these issues.

Nehruvian Secularism

In the first two decades after India's independence, the Nehruvian vision of secularism dominated the discourse. Being an atheist himself, he believed that the grip of religion over society would slacken with the modernization of society. Nehru being the architect of India and the most popular leader after the death of Gandhi, his vision became the guiding principles of the state policies. In retrospect, however, it can be safely argued that rising communal tensions even during his period belied his cardinal faith of rationality trumping religion. Just a decade after his death, vulnerability of secularism required constitutional codification. The term, secularism, was formally inserted in the Indian Constitution in 1976.

Contemporary Discourses and the Crisis of Secularism

Contemporary discourses on secularism are characterized by both continuities and discontinuities. The relevance of the Western secularity for the Indian context manifested partially in the Nehruvian vs. the Gandhian model of secularism continues to be debated. But a new dimension has been added by the modernization thesis and the notion of the 'Crisis of Secularism'.

On the issue of 'Western Secularity' which is based on the wall of separation thesis, i.e. separation of the church from the state, most Indian scholars argue that this is not relevant to the Indian context.[8] All three groups of left liberals, Gandhians and cultural determinists debunk that argument. Left liberals count on the virtues of the constitutional and Nehruvian approach of equidistance (or 'principled distance' as coined by Rajeev Bhargava) and respect for all religions; Gandhians advocate inter-religious harmony while the cultural determinists proclaim the grandeur of Hindutva as the basis of Indian nationalism.

Critiques of modernity (Ashis Nandy, T.N. Madan and Partha Chatterjee) consider secularism and communalism to be the product of some modern state practices. According to Nandy, to accept the ideology of secularism is to accept the ideology of progress and modernity as the new justification of domination and use the violence to achieve and sustain ideologies as the new opiates of the masses[9].

The Gandhian model of pre-modern and traditional forms of 'tolerance' which is based on the eclectic philosophy of Hinduism, Buddhism, Islam and Sikhism, is projected as a critique of the Nehruvian vision of secularism based on Western modernity and secularity. Two of the famous Bollywood Hindi songs reflect this contradiction: *Hindu, Muslim, Sikh, Ishai- ham sab hain bhai bhai* (Hindu, Muslim, Sikh and Christians are brothers) *vs. Na Hindu banega na musalman banega, insan ki aulad hai insan banega* (You will neither be Hindu, nor Muslim—as a child of a human, you will only be a human). The first song acknowledges the significance of religious identity of the person and advocates inter-religious harmony while the latter denounces this identity and extols the virtues of being human.

Cultural nationalists denounce the Nehruvian and the Congress model as 'pseudo-secularism'—aimed at appeasing Muslims and garnering their votes. They give the example of the Shah Bano Case of 1985, non-implementation of the Uniform Civil Code and so on. It is paradoxical that the 'crisis of secularism' is assumed to be real by both sides—those who share the Nehruvian vision of secularism and their opponents who endorse cultural nationalism[10]. The former refers to the disruption of harmony and religious equilibrium due to the rise of Hindu nationalism while the latter debase the Nehruvian secularism as 'pseudo-secularism' and opportunistic. The advocates of Hindu nationalism do not object to the value of secularism but they would like to have a different interpretation and meaning of secularism[11]. This rhetoric, however, is often belied by the practices of Hindu nationalists. This has led to the crisis of secularism in terms of its interpretation and state practices.

Conclusion

To sum up, secularism is a dynamic concept, the meaning of which is contingent upon the interaction between the state and religion in a particular context. In the case of India, we can see that one meaning of secularism has been contested by others. Its meaning has evolved over time and will continue to do so in future. As an analyst my duty was to bring forth some of the important discourses, and as a citizen, I will endorse the discourse on secularism which does not discriminate against people on the basis of religion and does not seek to homogenize the nation and, annihilate alternative discourses, literal or figurative.

NOTES

1. For details see Partha Chatterjee, 'Secularism and Tolerance' in Rajeev Bhargava (ed.) *Secularism and its Critics*, Oxford

University Press, New Delhi, 1998.

2. Ibid.
3. Ibid.
4. A brief summary of this debate has been provided by Shefali Jha, 'Secularism in the Constituent Assembly Debates, 1946-1950', *Economic and Political Weekly*, July 27, 2002. The Constituent Assembly debated the principle of secularism on October 17, 1949.
5. Ibid.
6. ibid.
7. ibid.
8. For distinctness of Indian secularism see Rajeev Bhargava in Rajeev Bhargava (ed.) *Secularism and its Critics*, Oxford University Press, New Delhi, 1998.
9. Ashis Nandy, 'The Politics of Secularism and the Recovery of Religious Tolerance' in Rajeev Bhargava (ed.) *Secularism and its Critics*, Oxford University Press, New Delhi, 1998.
10. Partha Chatterjee, 'Secularism and Tolerance' in Rajeev Bhargava (ed.) *Secularism and its Critics*, Oxford University Press, New Delhi, 1998.
11. Ibid.

9

Effects of New Media on Democracy

S.K. Ray

Media can be defined as the means of transmitting messages, thoughts, opinions and view points. The present-day world has witnessed fundamental changes in the media environment. Technologies and format innovations have created new ways of communicating and reaching audiences thus providing a new meaning and name to media—electronic/digital media.

Electronic Media

Electronic media uses electronics for the end-user audience to access the content. This is in contrast to static media (mainly print media), which today are most often created electronically, but do not require electronics to be accessed by the end-user in the printed form. The primary electronic media sources familiar to the general public are better known as video recordings, audio recordings, multimedia presentations, slide presentations, CD-ROM and online content. Most new media are in the form of digital media. Digital media is a form of electronic media where data are stored in digital (as opposed to analog) form. It can refer to the technical aspect of storage and transmission (e.g. hard disc drives or computer networking) of information or to the "end product", such as digital video, digital signage, digital audio, or digital art. Digital media is defined as "the creative convergence of digital arts, science, technology and business for human expression, communication, social interaction and education". The electronic media will be termed as new media in this presentation which includes Internet, social media like Facebook, Twitter, Linkedin and many others.

Reliance on the Internet

The Internet is a two-way street. It enables citizens to get and post information about politicians and it allows those politicians to get advice from the people in larger numbers.

This collective decision-making and problem-solving gives more power to the citizens and helps politicians make decisions faster. This creates a more productive society that can handle problems faster and more efficiently. There is more political information disseminated today through a vast diversity of sources than at any time in history. Political news is available for general audiences through network newscasts and real time news broadcasts. The wide range of available formats also permits information to be targeted at specific audiences segments, including those who traditionally have been under-represented in the political world.

Interactivity

One of the primary characteristics of the "new media" age is the interactivity that communications technologies facilitate among citizens, public officials, and media personnel. Rather than merely being passive recipients of political information, it is now possible for citizens to make their political presence and opinions known, and to play a more visible role in political events.

Empowerment of Individuals

People who have an interest in current political issues and the capacity to learn about them now have access to the information they need to be equipped to make an impact on public policy. Using online tools to organize, people can more easily be involved in the policy-making process of government. The first impact has also led to a greater amount of public engagement efforts. Government officials are pressured by more highly informed, opinionated, and potentially effective citizens to make more of an effort to address the public's concerns.

The lower cost of information exchange on the Internet, as well as the high level of reach that the content potentially has, makes the Internet an attractive medium for political information.

For example, environmental or social issue groups may find the Internet an easier mechanism to increase awareness of their issues, compared to traditional media outlets, such as television or newspapers, which require heavy financial investment.

Democracy and the Implementation of the Internet

In order to have a democratic, free nation, all information that can be shared, should be shared. The Internet works towards an "informationalization" of society and everyday life through increasing democratic demands. The Internet, specifically social media sites provide information, facilitate communication and interactions, and allow for intellectual and physical transactions to be made.

A. The Internet provides a sense of relevance in participation through allowing everyone's voice to be heard and expressed.
B. A structure of social inclusion is also provided

through a wide variety of Internet sites, groups, and social networks, all representing different viewpoints and ideas.

C. Sensitivity to the individual's needs is accomplished through the ability to express individual opinions publicly and rapidly.

D. Finally, the Internet is an extremely flexible area of participation; it is low in cost and widely available to the public.

Through these four directions, democracy and the implementation of the Internet are able to play an active role in societal change.

Societies are transforming from a system based on group control to one of "networked individualism". These networked societies are constructed post -"triple revolution" of technology, which involves a three step process. Step one in the "triple revolution" is "the turn to social networks", step two: "the proliferation of the far-flung, instantaneous internet", and step three: "the even wider proliferation of always-available mobile phones".

These elements play a key role in change through the Internet. Such technologies provide an alternative sphere that is unregulated by the government, and where construction of ideas and protests can foster without regulation.

Internet also plays a central role in deliberative democracy, where deliberation and access to multiple viewpoints is central in decision-making. Internet is able to provide an opportunity for interaction, and serves as a prerequisite in the deliberative process as a research tool. On the Internet the exchange of ideas is widely encouraged through a vast number of websites, blogs, and social networking outlets, such as Twitter; all of which encourage freedom of expression. Through the Internet information is easily accessible, and in a cost-effective manner, providing access and means for change.

Benefits, Disadvantages and Challenges

Information and communication technologies are neither democratic nor undemocratic; they are merely means to an end and not normative by their nature.

Disadvantages

Illiteracy and digital divide between those with access to the new media of democracy (mobile phones and Internet connections) and those without, as well as the opportunity cost of expenditure on e-democracy innovations are the major obstacle in mass participation.

5. Challenges

To provide inclusive access to the Internet and other communication channels is indeed a challenge. This is a fundamental democracy issue. If the Internet is to become a new democratic tool, through which people can participate in and influence the democratic process, it is vital that everyone who wants irrespective of age, gender, profession or geographical location – has the physical access to it and the skills and confidence to use it.

Security and the protection of privacy. The government must be in a position to guarantee, where appropriate, that online communications are secure and that they do not violate people's privacy.

Diffusion of new democracy is also hampered by hostile political environments, dictatorial regimes and anti-democratic forces. It has become common for governments to implement Internet crackdowns during times of widespread political protests.

Profit Motives

The imperative behind political communication in the current era is profit, and not a sense of public service. The public can be dissatisfied with the political media offerings. A majority of citizens believe that the news is unduly influenced by powerful business and political interests who play into the media's own desire to make profits.

10

Socialism STR and Social Revolution in India

Ramesh Rattan

Socialism which becomes the most inspiring word in human history had gained roots in India after the Soviet/Bolshevik Revolution of 1917. It has substituted the slogan of the French Revolution of liberty, equality and fraternity. In fact our history is the struggle between continually developing forces of production and stagnated system of social management.

The slogan of socialism, after 70 years of its existence and changing the civilization on this planet in an unprecedented manner, has lost its guiding and inspiring shine. The command system with the centralized economy could not meet with the aspirations of the people adopting it. On the other hand, the theory of free economy propounded by capitalists is facing a crises on such a scale that most of the people on this globe want to change this mode of production/distribution which exploit our natural resources in a ruthless manner causing misery to a wider section of toiling masses.

We are trying to formulate a system of our social management to fulfil our aspiration of equality and justice. Where every member of our society can enjoy the benefits brought to us by scientific development and hard earned management. Where no one should be deprived of basic necessities and creativity is not crippled. Where greed is controlled and natural sources are explored. We should establish a new way of relationship with nature. Being a conscious element on this earth we feel duty bound and want to protect our nature by exploring new ways to start a two way and balancing cycle.

In our pursuit to find a new system in political superstructure and economic structure we have to adopt a new approach to perceive and analyse the facts. The basic philosophy of dialectical materialism propounded by Karl Marx is still relevant but we cannot dogmatically follow all his propositions in the political or economic field because productive forces have changed qualitatively and quantitatively from that time. We have to adopt Lenin's method based on the deductive method because inductive or priory methods of analysis in this situation can derail us to some other subjective type of conclusions.

The development in science, technology and communication has not only changed the way of production of things but every step in STR has dynamically affected society to change its way of living, information, thinking, socialization and in many other ways (interacting, a esthetically, culturally, through entertainment, etc). This is a universal phenomena and no country or nation can remain aloof from its dynamic affects.

The worrying affect of STR is that it had turned our nature from infinity to a limited entity. None of the above mentioned political systems (capitalism or socialism) had taken care of the deteriorating condition and potentiality of nature. The realities of our time want us to include these environmental costs and social costs in our costing system. The capitalists with their existing bent of mind resist these costing theories vehemently. The socialists could be made to agree to this and they can lead this movement to save the earth.

This type of development has caused the emergence of giant cities and metropolises. The urbanization is a new but rapidly growing phenomenon. It has its own problems related with transportation, drinking water, sewerage and disposals, law and order and governance, parking, playgrounds, schools and health services, entertainment and relaxing spaces.

The progressive systems/new systems have to develop their industries and habitation in a different but logically convincing manner. They have to fulfil the requirement and aspirations of their people in a developed and transparent manner. There also exist some other problems like war, drugs, etc. on this earth which demand to be resolved through international forums. The progressive forces have to develop different ways of industrialization and urbanization where the load on non-renewable natural sources is reduced considerably to a tolerant level of preserving the natural cycles.

India is a developing country. Patriots of this country have made many sacrifices for the liberation and betterment of its people. We have some very good economic and political institutions and traditions to feel proud of. In the political field our constitution, right to vote, parliamentary system, independence of judiciary, relatively independent office and department of CAG and Election Commission are the basis for our future growth.

In the economy we have various structures with diverse relations. A times they supplement each other on some other point having an antagonistic approach towards contending entities. We have the public sector providing us basic and heavy industry, railways, banks, telecommunications, government institutes of technology and management.

We have big corporate houses developed by skilful integration of technologies and management. They have formed a major part of our productive forces. We cannot ignore their role in the production of commodities required by our vast population. They have many means at their disposal. Big industrial houses are controlled by highly skilled technocrats and managers and some of them have even their own estates and institutions for education and health. They are easily capable of influencing governments, media, political parties and NGOs.

Then there are medium and small-scale and micro industries.

We have various agricultural as well as service sectors.

Our economies are not only divided on the scale of production but also these are divided according to region and community. There also exist some intervening economies.

Every section has contributed to the building of this nation. Efforts must be made to give due place to the interest and views of every section. Then there is lop-sided development in industry and trade.

The present industrial and urban structures are complex in nature. They need a highly skilled management to control and it can easily tend to lead to the centralization of power and that can lead to dictatorship. There can be no dictatorship if efforts are made to cater to the need of every section of society.

Democracy has to be adopted as our way of thinking and living. Democracy is not simply a right to oppose but in fact it is adjusting the divergent view for further development. It is a tool of integration of various views, culture, habits, intellect, skill and traditions for further development.

We need a new type of conglomeration of state and civil society able to regulate and control powerful corporates, able to facilitate other fragile structures in the economy, able to generate balance in various economic sectors and structures, regions and sections of population, able to address the problems of environment and natural sources. It is only socialism with a democratic approach or democracy moving towards socialism can secure our future. It will be better if we substitute it with democratic pluralism because in our country a nation with so much diversity cannot move with any kind of centralism. Neither democratic centralism nor socialistic centralism is able to fulfil our aspirations. Pluralistic management in production of commodities adjusting itself according to the taste and culture of different regions and sections has already begun to deliver good results. Our political management seriously requires political democratic pluralism. We have to choose the method of assimilation of positivity of various fields, sectors, sections and regions.

Fundamentalism and sectarianism of any kind are hazardous for development.

11

Communal Fascism: A Threat to Democracy

C. Ganesh Pandian

Democracy is a form of government in which people are governed by their own elected representatives. Abraham Lincoln, the sixteenth President of the United States of America, aptly defined democracy as a government of the people, by the people and for the people. This definition clearly underlines the basic tenet that, in this form of government, people are supreme. The ultimate power is in their hands and they exercise it in the form of electing their representatives during the elections. Democracy entered its golden stage in the 20th century. Many countries in the world today follow the democratic form of government. Democracy depends on the following conditions:

- coexistence of ideas and of parties;
- the right to free discussion;
- universal adult suffrage; and
- periodic elections.

Democracy in India

India is the biggest democracy in the world, with a population of over one billion. India, a union of states, is a sovereign socialist, secular, democratic, republic, with a parliamentary system of government. The republic is governed in terms of the Constitution, which was adopted on November 26, 1949 and came into force on January 26, 1950. During the past sixty-five years there have been regular elections to the Parliament and state legislatures. This reflects the maturity and wisdom of the Indian electorate, in whom the ultimate power and sovereignty rests. With the passage of time, Indian voters have become more assertive and active regarding their participation in the process of democracy. The turnout of Indian voters has significantly increased during the past elections. This phenomenon reflects the growing political awareness and maturity of the Indian masses, which, in turn, has made the various political parties more conscious of their responsibility and accountability to the people.

Fundamental Rights Under Democracy

Liberty, equality, justice and fraternity are the very cornerstones of democracy. They are not available under dictatorship and utilitarian forms of government. Without *freedom of speech, expression of faith, profession, and association,* democracy is meaningless. The Indian Constitution offers all Indian citizens, individually and collectively, these basic freedoms and rights. They are guaranteed in the Constitution in the form of six broad categories of Fundamental Rights and are justifiable.

It means that each and every Indian citizen has the right to constitutional remedies for the enforcement of these rights. There is a free, independent and separate judiciary to ensure that these rights are not violated and tampered with. This is the very spirit and essence of our democracy. An independent, strong and incorruptible judiciary is one of the main pillars of democracy.

Further Indian democratic states and its governing

institutions like political executive, Parliament and judiciary have to act as 'guardians' of the freedoms guaranteed to the Indian citizens by the Constitution. Indian citizens have enjoyed freedom along with restrictions imposed by the Indian state and laws like the *Preventive Detention Act, Maintenance of Internal Security Act, Prevention of Terrorist Act and Other Special Security Laws* have been in operation from the very beginning under Indian democracy. The concept of national security and rights and liberties of citizens are bound to come into conflict with each other. Thus an independent judiciary, National Human Rights Commission and a vigilant press act as guardians and defenders of freedoms against arbitrariness of state functionaries.

The Supreme Court of India in the case of the *People's Union for Civil Liberties v. Union of India (2003)* stated that '*It is established that the fundamental rights themselves have no fixed content, most of them are empty vessels into which each generation must pour its content in the light of its fundamental rights by process of judicial interpretation to keep young, energetic and alive*'. A major issue is that the citizens often do not have the power to defend their freedoms and rights from the authorities of the state who decide to cripple rights in the name of defence of national security and arrest citizens by denying them the right to defend themselves under laws which permit 'detention without trial'. At present under the neoliberal framework fundamental rights especially the rights like the right to freedom of speech and expression Article 19(1)(a) and the various freedoms under Articles 14, 19 and 21 are given a go by.

Communalism and Democracy in India

Communalism, as we understand it in our country is blind loyalty to one's own religious group. It is described as a tool to mobilize people for or against by raising an appeal on communal lines.

Communalism is associated with religious fundamentalism and dogmatism. According to Asghar Ali Engineer, *"it is an instrument in the hands of the upper class to concentrate power by dividing people"*. The elites strive to maintain a status quo against transformation by dividing people on communal and religious lines. Communalism may be perceived as a total commitment to a set of beliefs that are far from rationality. Indian society is pluralistic from the religious point of view. Here, we have the followers of all the great religious systems. Hindus constitute the bulk of the population and they live in all parts of the country. Muslims constitute the largest religious minority.

In the communal riots during the period of independence millions of people were rendered homeless while millions of others lost their property. Communalism was responsible for the division of the country into India and Pakistan. The partition was expected to resolve the riddle, but it failed. There is, yet, to develop the neighbourhood living pattern between Hindus and Muslims.

Reasons for Communal Riots

The reasons for the existence and continuation of communal riots are as follows:

- The riots are part of progress in an underdeveloped country. The class struggle is converted into a communal struggle weakening the solidarity of the proletariat class.
- The middle and backward classes have acquired greater political and economic strength and influence and these often assert themselves.

These above explanations cannot be binding. Often economic reasons emerge after (not before) the rioting has begun. Again in a developing society economic factors where competitive or one lagging behind the other can lead to a riot.

Remedies

It is essential to seek the factors which can remedy the communal divide in India. Some suggestions are:

- First, religion should be separated from politics and communal bodies should be banned.
- Second, the freedom of the press should not extend to spreading communal ideas.
- Communalism needs to be denounced by political leaders and all leading citizens.
- Measures should be taken for raising the economic lot of the minority community.
- Steps should be taken that lead to peace between communities and an end to communal violence.
- Community leaders should explain the situation to the community and defuse tensions.
- Religion should not become the whipping boy of political ambitions.

Communalism to Communal Fascism

Apart from the above remedies it should be noted that communalism in India at present has attained the stage of communal fascism which could be described as a situation in which the communal and majoritarian ideas have collaborated with the neoliberal framework of the state. They have penetrated into various parts inside the state machinery. Whenever corporate capitalism finds it difficult to achieve the desired results it smashes the democratic set up of the state and establishes a fascist state in its place. India's present position is at the crossroads. The fascist threat is threatening people especially the progressive and democratic minded ones. It is the duty of the progressive and leftist sections of our country to defeat the propaganda of these communal forces and uphold the ideals of secularism and socialism.

12

The Political Significance of 'Social Media Networks'

M. Vijaya Kumar

The popular protests witnessed from Turkey to Brazil recently and in the Arab world for quite some time have one aspect in common—growing dissent among not only the working class and peasantry, who are waging struggles against exploitation, marginalization and denial of basic rights, but also the young, educated and better-off sections protesting against the very system that once enriched them. The governments see this as a great danger. It is said that social media such as Facebook, Twitter, Skype and smart-phones are being used as tools to bring about change. Can Facebook or Twitter trigger and win a revolution? This is a popular common misconception, being peddled and circulated by the mass media. We should not forget that technology by itself cannot bring about a change. But the application of these tools of technology for an intended constructive purpose, can only become an agent of change. The physical conditions for this phenomenon have emerged in recent times.

India's Realities

Most regions of the world, developed and developing alike, are seeing the rapid rise of the use of social networking sites and smart-phone technologies. There are an estimated 240 crore users of Internet and 500 crore users of cell phones in the world. Nearly 80 per cent of Indians now have a mobile phone, but only 11 per cent have Internet access, and fewer than 5 per cent use social media. There are 65 million Facebook users and an estimated 35 million Twitter accounts. In rural areas, these percentages are significantly lower. Social media is still confined to the upper crust of the population: the affluent, educated, English-speaking youth of India's major cities. In India, those who use social media are more likely to live in cities, hold a passport, and international contacts. In the remote towns, villages, and slums, most residents remain disconnected from social media. In spite of the conscious promotion of social media and other modern communication technologies as weapons of change, social media cannot replace organization on the ground, in slums and villages. That is the most important factor for working in India.

As much as 70 per cent of India's population lives in rural areas and 52 per cent of the nation's workforce are engaged in agriculture and allied activities, while agriculture accounts for only 13.7 per cent of the nation's gross domestic product (GDP) as of now. India has 50 crores of young people. Out of 70 crores of working age population, only 48 crores are employed in some sort of occupation and the rest are without any regular and reliable source of income. Employment in the unorganized sector accounts for 91.39 per cent of workforce. Working conditions in most of these enterprises is appalling, inhuman and the work is unremunerative. Large industries are no longer employment generators. The neoliberal mantra of "zero employment growth" coupled with automation is wreaking havoc with the employment generation capability of the Indian economy.

Many irresponsible politicians and intellectuals claim

that since agriculture employs half the population, but contributes only one-seventh of the nation's wealth, it is imperative that at least 30 crores of people have to leave agriculture and seek other means of livelihood. This is what we are witness to as the population of cities is exploding, what with people thrown out of their livelihoods in the rural areas, congregating to cities and are forced to live in slums, seeking work that is scarce to find. But the moot question is that with almost a third of the people of working age in the country unemployed or underemployed, how can a few urban centres absorb such a huge influx of displaced rural population? It is frightening to realize that the right combination of ingredients for social unrest is in place and a catastrophe can occur any day.

The Significance of Globalization

As Karl Marx stated, the development of the productive forces could never be looked at in isolation from the class character of this development. The term "development" has almost become synonymous with the achievement of a high rate of growth of the gross domestic product (GDP). As we know, high GDP growth has not been producing jobs. This is bound to happen under capitalist production in the long run, since capitalists are motivated by profitability and are prepared to dispense with hiring labour completely if a machine can do the job and give them higher profits. Countries with large labour reserves like India and China can never solve their unemployment problem without active measures to support agricultural production and follow labour-intensive growth strategies, which are anathema to capitalists.

Changes brought about by globalization and neo-liberalism have resulted in the growing separation of individuals from traditional bases of social solidarity such as family ties, local gatherings, political parties, places of worship, and other kinds of mass organizations. Individuals are increasingly getting isolated from society and the reality around them. Elderly people constantly complain that the present generation spends most of its time conversing on their cell or smart phones and iPads, busying themselves with the social media. They appear to be least bothered about what is going on around them, their families' travails and tribulations and in the immediate political sphere. They exhibit a disdain for everything that happens around them.

Shattered Dreams

Indeed, the early 21st century has given rise to a new sociological category: middle class and working class, young adults with limited horizons. These are young people with education but with bleak employment prospects. Most of them, the world over, are living in societies where youth forms a substantial share of the population, plagued by high wealth disparities, high unemployment rates and bleak prospects of gaining any livelihood. It is reported that in our country, only ten per cent of graduates and postgraduates who leave their colleges can expect to gain employment. In the case of professional graduates, this number is around 15-20 per cent. Even if they manage to get a job, it is neither secure nor remunerative. For example, an average engineering graduate can expect a temporary job paying around Rs. 10-15,000 monthly, if he is fortunate. Compare this with those few lucky ones who get selected for an IT job with a remuneration of around Rs. 30-50,000, but with no job guarantee. The really fortunate few are those who manage to get a government or PSU job with a starting pay anywhere between Rs. 40-50,000 to start, with lifetime security. I once addressed a gathering of 500 engineering students. I was curious to know how they look at the world and asked them about the biggest problem they face in their lives. I got a resounding unanimous response, "we have no future! We cannot get a job once we leave college!" They are technologically savvy and navigate the virtual world with ease. With the neoliberal model failing to deliver its promise, reality is biting back on the young generation with revenge.

The country's youth are increasingly getting atomized, being deprived of living contacts with the society around them, what with the poor quality of education imparted to them, making them blissfully unaware of their cultural and social roots. They have become passive recipients of neo-liberal propaganda and are slaves of consumer culture. Neoliberalism is replacing our democracy with a corporatocracy, replacing critical thinking citizens with citizens who are more inclined to shop than vote, replacing care for others with excessive greed, replacing equal opportunity with opportunities only for the wealthy, rewriting laws to favour corporations and the extremely wealthy, converting the middle class to the new poor, and presenting youth, especially minority youth, as an internal security threat rather than a key ingredient in the infrastructure of our democracy.

Once the reality strikes back at them and they are left high and dry by the system, they suddenly find themselves deprived of any moral social support. This explains the alarming increase in suicides among the youth.

When these young people have no other option, but to come into the streets and protest against the system and fight its injustice, the methods employed for gathering support have changed radically. Political pandits routinely declare that the 'Me' generation is only interested in their own well-being and find no need to participate in any social activity, other than indulging in chatting, Facebook and Twitter and visiting pubs. This kind of a social behaviour of the youth suits the interests of powers that be and big business. But in the last few years, the picture has undergone a dramatic change. We find more and more urban youth coming out into the streets protesting against injustice.

Why people back a cause is based on many factors and relates to what is happening in the day-to-day world. With prices rising and falling living standards, unbridled corruption and misuse of power by the elite holding power, working people and youth are increasingly resorting to street action to voice their grievances, which was considered impossible twenty years ago, what with capitalism appearing victorious and the trumpeting of the rich that 'There Is No Alternative (TINA)'. What we are witnessing today is indeed a revolution of sorts, shattering the myth of TINA. Even the middle classes and better off working classes also supported the capitalists for the last 20 years. But it is no longer the case. All over the world, the resounding answer to TINA, "Another World Is Possible" is gaining supporters, especially from the youth and downtrodden. This is evident from the rise of progressive and anti-capitalist regimes elected democratically to power in Latin America and the growing popularity of anti-capitalist parties and groups in countries like Germany, Greece, Spain and Portugal in Europe. This is the structural shift that took place, especially in the last decade.

Can Facebook and Twitter Bring About a Revolution?

But the fact is that, at the ground level, a revolution is a remote possibility, in fact more than what we see and hear on the Internet and mass media. It requires years of painstaking and sustained effort at organizing, background work, funding and building up mass appeal and personal sacrifices. As seen from the experiences of mass movements in the Arab world and Brazil among other places, we understand from reports and analyses that it was not simply the social media that had brought hundreds of thousands of people into the streets and got them involved in prolonged protests, daring police brutality and repression. A lot was also achieved through word of mouth—people propagating their ideas and appeal for action in their local communities.

It is not simply the social media by itself that is bringing out and mobilizing people, but it is important to understand that this movement builds on a legacy of protest by many different grassroots organizations, most of which are not significantly represented online. Every mass movement needs spaces where political alternatives can be debated and organization can take place. As one of the Brazilian protesters in Rio had said, "There were many catalysts of the uprising."

The activists in Egypt have reported that nearly three decades of underground organization against many odds and repression by the state, was carried out by political parties, trade unions and other social organizations, who had built up the awareness of people. That explains why people have ventured out on to the streets when the decisive moment arrived.

New communications, infrastructures and technologies are not the only ones triggering the protests we are seeing, but they are probably making them easier. Online tools such as Facebook are not so much creating new forms of protest as amplifying traditional forms of protest, such as street demonstrations. Social media allow organizers to involve like-minded people in a movement at a very low cost, but they do not necessarily make these people move. Social media are tools that allow revolutionary groups to lower the costs of participation, organization, recruitment and training. In other words, activism does not confine itself to separate online and offline spheres, but instead online interactions can aid offline forms of people's participation. Social media represents only one tool among many for an opposition group to utilize. Protest movements are rarely successful if led from the safety of people's homes. There should be leaders with charisma and be street smart, just like leaders of any organization.

A small, but well funded group of IT professionals is working hard to garner support to Narendra Modi, the BJP's prime ministerial candidate in the upcoming general elections in 2014. Though it is of concern to all secular and democratic forces and has to be countered with determination, it is to be seen to what extent they will succeed in garnering the support of middle class youth, who are avid users of social media, what with the political equations changing rapidly with the entry of new forces such as AAP.

But like any tool, social media has inherent weaknesses and strengths. Their effectiveness depends on how effectively the leaders identify themselves with the people and how accessible they are to the youth who are brought in because of the ideas they identify themselves with through their use of social media. To lead a protest movement effectively, an organization's leadership has to venture outside cyberspace. It has to learn what it means to face a regime's counter intelligence capabilities both in the virtual and real worlds. By educating and raising the consciousness of the target population, the leadership of a movement learns the different strategies that work best with different social strata and how to appeal to a broad audience. Moreover, a leadership grounded in physical reality is one that constructs and sticks to a concerted plan of action.

People, not social media, remain the drivers of social change. But as public debate is broadened through the use of instruments like social media, this can potentially lead to positive political and social change in the real world. The key for any protest movement is to inspire and motivate individuals to go from the comfort of their homes to the chaos of the streets and face the disturbing insecurity of fighting against the government. In fact, the middle classes abhor insecurity and avoid like the plague anything that threatens their perceived security. Now, they have no alternative left as what they consider their secure life to be falling apart.

If the right conditions exist and a revolution can occur, the social media can play a catalytic role. Just because an Internet-based group for agitation is launched, it does not automatically make it popular or a threat. There are Facebook groups, YouTube videos and Twitter posts about everything, right from extremist groups to surreptitious groups that eschew fascist ideologies, but that does not make them popular. The climate must be ripe for revolution. We can now watch a protest movement developing and shaping up in real time, instead of the reports filed and printed in the following day's newspaper or broadcast on the nighttime news. Social media has become an important instrument for activists to spread information that their government wants to prevent from flowing. Since the traditional media did not cover the protests, social media became an important source of information and elevated its role into a political issue.

We find protest participants using images captured on their cell phones and then broadcasting to millions on satellite TV to change public opinion in profound ways. Police atrocities on the protestors are usually suppressed in the mass media, but the new technologies enable the protest movements to reach millions of people across the world directly using social media. In the process, innovative visualizations emerge that capture the spread of protests across Facebook, Twitter, Youtube and other social media platforms such as Tumblr, Instagram, and Whatsapp. These spontaneous efforts underline the transformative effects of technology in shaping a digital revolution.

Promoting Change Through Social Media

The huge public awareness brought on by the Delhi Gang-Rape case in India and all over the world is undeniable. The sustained social media discussions helped to build up pressure on the Indian government, prompting it to set up several safety measures and deterrents.

If thousands of youths, among others, hit the streets of Delhi to express their anger against inaction of the establishment, it is not without planning, after all. As most of them are already members of famous social organizations such as women, youth and student organizations, use of networking sites, such as Facebook (FB) and Twitter greatly added to the communication of any message to be spread.

Activist Anna Hazare's popular anti-corruption movement, which was also likened by the media to the Arab Spring had served a limited purpose. As a tool for communication, the social media, including social networking sites, is still in its nascent stage.

Countering Social Media by the Establishments

Many governments are finding it increasingly difficult to counter and control the public protests in a world where information is available in real-time, and at an enormous scale. They can no longer use the official media to dictate what the people should hear, see and think. In fact, government controlled media like Doordarshan have lost their appeal long ago.

On the other hand, social media can quickly turn into a valuable intelligence-collection tool for the governments.

Beyond monitoring movement websites, governments can also shut them down. Social media undoubtedly offer advantages in disseminating messages quickly and broadly, but they are also vulnerable to government control tactics. And while the effectiveness of the tool depends on the quality of a movement's leadership, a dependence only on social media can actually prevent good leadership from developing.

Regimes can also use social media for their own purposes. The ever enlarging cyber discussions about 'Occupy Wall Street' is creating an evolving database of raw information about the leaderless protest movement, a potential tool for those seeking to anticipate its next step. The US authorities use this information to track down radical elements behind the movement. One counter-protest tactic employed by the governments is to spread disinformation. The recent reports of the US authorities employing the NSA to monitor every message and interaction the world over, is an example of this.

Lessons for the Indian Left

The Indian Left has to effectively use the social media to spread their message and mobilize public opinion. In fact, we find efforts in this direction with leftist cadres actively involving themselves in social media. This is also opening up a new dimension in the leftist movement. The normal method of disseminating information and taking feedback in political organizations with "Democratic Centralism" is through reports disseminated from above and in the party's official organs. But now, the matrix of information flow and counter flow is opening up new avenues for party cadres to get exposed to and express their views on a number of contemporary issues, which otherwise go unheard. Today it is possible for activists to file reports about their movements and also post photographs and videos online, so that their comrades in other regions can access this information and disseminate it among the cadres, thus enhancing mutual inspiration.

The other important aspect is that when party leaders indulge in discussions on the social media, they are forced to explain their stand on issues, which otherwise is possible only through official channels. It is a welcome development that leftist political leaders have ventured into social media. From my experience, I understand that dedicated party cadres are not shy of criticizing their party leadership on many issues on the social media. This is a new opening for debate and I am sure will lead the way for a fresh mindset among leftist parties. It is also possible for the party leadership to guide any movement from a distance in real time, while getting reports, pictures and videos and guiding their local leaders to counter the enemy at the most crucial moments.

The present mass media, controlled by big business naturally prevents the message of the Left Parties from reaching the people. In many instances, they spread false information. But social media is widely accessible to the public and we can effectively use this vital tool to amplify our agitational efforts. But in the end, we should not forget the social media is at best an enabler of the people's movement and cannot in any case replace mass action.

List of Contributors

Anil Rajimwale, General Secretary, AIPF.

Bharat Bhushan Prasad, retired computer scientist in JNU, New Delhi.

C. Ganesh Pandian, social activist.

C.R. Bakshi, Coordinator, Akhil Bharatiya Adivasi Masabha (ABAM). A veteran freedom fighter and expert in labour problems.

Krishna Jha, researcher and journalist.

M. Aravind Kumar, Associate Professor, Chennai.

M. Vijaya Kumar, retired Assistant General Manager in BHEL (Hyderabad), headed projects in India, Saudi Arabia, etc, presently writing on ancient Indian philosophy, reputed world scientist. Presently Working President, AIPF.

Rajan Kumar, Professor, School of International Studies, Jawaharlal Nehru University, New Delhi.

Ramesh Rattan, entrepreneur, leading figure of the Small Scale Traders' and Manufacturers' Association in Ludhiana and Punjab, specialist in problems of small-scale industry.

S.K. Ray, social activist and independent researcher.

Soma S. Marla, world renowned geneticist, scientist with various research institutes in India and abroad. Active in social concerns, especially in farmers' problems.

Yugal Rayalu, Professor in Electrical Engineering (Maharashtra), post-doctorate in English Literature, specialist in religious philosophy, especially Christianity.